THE *Spirit-* CONTROLLED WOMAN

Beverly LaHaye

HARVEST HOUSE PUBLISHERS
Eugene, Oregon 97402

THE SPIRIT-CONTROLLED WOMAN

Copyright © 1995 by Harvest House Publishers
Eugene, Oregon 97402

Library of Congress Cataloging-in-Publication Data

LaHaye, Beverly.
      The Spirit-controlled woman / Beverly LaHaye.
        p.   cm.
      Originally published: Irvine, Calif. : Harvest House, ©1976.
      ISBN 1-56507-223-5 (Trade)
      ISBN 1-56507-404-1 (Hardcover)
      1. Women—Conduct of life.   2. Women—Religious life.   3. Holy Spirit.
   I. Title.
   BJ1610.L2   1994   94-29312
   248.8'43—dc20   CIP

Printed in the United States of America.

95   96   97   98   99   00   01   02   —   10   9   8   7   6   5   4   3   2   1

ACKNOWLEDGMENTS

Most major projects are not completed by just one person. The dream, vision, and writing of the book was my part. But the typing, editing, and watching for deadlines can be attributed to two faithful assistants: Kelly Gegner and Marion Wallace.

Last, but not at all least, I want to thank my husband, Tim LaHaye, for being available at any time and serving as my consultant. We all pray this book will be a blessing to many.

CONTENTS

FOREWORD

Dearest Bev,

For years I have been asked to write a book on temperament and the Spirit-filled life from the woman's point of view. I have recognized the need for such a work, but my problem is, I don't think like a woman. That job needed to be done by a member of the "fairer sex." Obviously that leaves me out.

When Bob Hawkins Sr. urged you to write such a book, I heartily agreed for two reasons. For years you have been immersed in the concept of the four temperaments, and I can testify that since you surrendered yourself completely to God some 13 years ago, your temperament has been controlled by the Holy Spirit. I have witnessed a sweet, soft-spirited worry machine who was afraid of her own shadow be transformed into a gracious, outgoing, radiant woman. Through this transformation and the lectures you have given on the Spirit-filled life, God has used you to inspire thousands of women to accept Him and the abundant life He offers.

It has been fun watching you burn the midnight oil writing this book. Thirteen years ago you would have been frightened off the first page. Now you have trusted Him who is able to do exceedingly abundantly above all that we can ask or think— and it is finished.

I think you've done a great job and will join you in prayer that the concepts you have shared so effectively through your public ministry will now bless thousands more through the reading of this book. I will also pray that many of them will enjoy the same transformation you have.

To be very honest, I prefer the new Beverly. Oh, I've always loved you; after all, I'm commanded to! But since you became a Spirit-filled woman, I find you much more exciting and easier to love. I have a hunch other husbands will have the same experience after their wives learn the joys of being a

Spirit-Controlled Woman. I sure thank God for sending you into my life!

With all my love,

Tim

(written in 1976)

P.S. Many years have passed since I wrote the above words, and the story is incredibly better. Little did we dream back then that God would recognize your deep concern for the moral and cultural decline in our nation and lead you to start Concerned Women for America. Today, you—a former "fearful woman"—serve as president of the largest pro-family women's organization in the country. You have established yourself as a respected Christian leader in Washington, as one who knows and has worked with U.S. presidents, cabinet members, senators, and congressmen, and who has even appeared before the Senate Judiciary Committee to testify on behalf of three Supreme Court nominees—an unbelievably scary environment. On top of that, you have birthed a daily radio talk show here in the nation's capital that now is the largest of its kind led by a woman and is carried to almost every city in the nation. You have proven in your life that God truly is "able to supply all our needs" if we just step out by faith and follow His leading. I admire the fact that you never limited God by unbelief. And best of all, you have not lost your gracious, Christlike spirit. I loved you back then, but I love you even more today.

1

The Beginning of a Richer Life

hy did some of my other friends seem to have more ability and potential than I had? How could God use me when there seemed to be something missing in my life? Could He ever use me for His glory? These were the questions that seemed to penetrate my heart in my first 15 years as a young wife of a minister.

Then one day I found the answer to those questions. This fearful and introverted person came face-to-face with the missing dimension in her life. Missing was the confidence and self-assuredness that "I can do all things through Christ who strengthens me" (Philippians 4:13). The constant fear of not being able to live up to other people's expectations, including my husband's, had haunted me on a regular basis. But through Christ, I gained confidence and overcame all those fears.

Well, I agreed to tell my story some 13 years later. It became the book published in 1976 called *The Spirit-Controlled Woman*, and it was straight from my heart. I wanted other women who might be struggling with some of the same emotions to know how God had worked in my life. There must have been many who were searching because, as the years have passed, over 800,000 copies of the book have been sold. But the years have a way of bringing maturity and wisdom. When those years are spent learning to walk in the Spirit and under the control of the Spirit, there has to be a richer understanding of our faith in Christ.

That is why I am now revising *The Spirit-Controlled Woman*. The basic message is the same because it is from the Word of God, but the depth of communicating those principles of the Word that can change our lives, is, I trust, much richer.

> *I needed power, love, and a sound mind to enable me to throw off my poor self-image and fear, step forward with new confidence, and let God do whatever He chose to do with my life.*

Before that experience I mentioned earlier, I had been a fearful, introverted person with a rather poor self-image. As a young wife, I was constantly fearful of not living up to the expectations of our friends. It was difficult for me to entertain in our home, and I refused most invitations to speak to women's groups because I felt so inadequate. I questioned if I really had anything to say to them. After all, who wants to hear what a young woman has to say whose only accomplishment in life was giving birth to four children? (Today I believe that is one of my greatest achievements and blessings.) One very well-meaning lady said to me in the early days of our ministry, "Mrs. LaHaye, our last pastor's wife was an author, and what do you do?" That was a heavy question for a fearful 27-year-old woman to cope with. But I began to wonder, "What did I do?" Yes, I was a good mother to my four children. I could keep house reasonably well, and my husband adored me. But what could I do that would be eternally effective in the lives of other women? The answer seemed to come back to me, "Very little!"

My first encounter with facing my mounting insecurities occurred at a Christian conference at Forest Home, California, in 1963. I heard Dr. Henry Brandt, a Christian psychologist, give a message about the filling of the Holy Spirit and the effect it could have on my life. This was the first time it had been presented to me so clearly, and instantly I recognized it as the missing dimension.

The fear and anxieties that possessed me were not from God: "For God has not given us a spirit of fear, but of power and of love and of a sound mind" (2 Timothy 1:7). This was exactly what I lacked! I needed power, love, and a sound mind to enable me to throw off my poor self-image and fear, step forward with new confidence, and let God do whatever He chose to do with my life. I knew my limitations and that I could only do this by turning the controls over to the Holy Spirit.

It was also helpful when I realized that I was wrong in not accepting myself as God had created me: "I will praise You, for I am fearfully and wonderfully made; marvelous are Your works, and that my soul knows very well" (Psalm 139:14).

Dr. Brandt talked to me about confessing my fears and anxieties as sin, "for whatever is not from faith is sin" (Romans 14:23b), and then asking to be filled with the Holy Spirit. I followed that simple formula and trusted the Holy Spirit over the days and months ahead to do the impossible through me because of this new power within me.

I will admit that there was no outward sign or expression except for a beautiful and quiet peace that settled in my heart. God was beginning to do a work in me that would be far more effective than anything I could do myself. I wanted to do the impossible for God. My new discovery did not change me overnight, in a week, or even in a month. But as I began to daily draw on that power, love, and sound mind, God was working within me. The missing dimension had been found. My natural temperament was still a part of me, but God was going to work on my weaknesses. Together we would see a transformed Beverly begin to grow.

My testimony is that I have come this far by faith and the power of the Holy Spirit. I still have a long way to go, but God is faithfully working in me to prepare me for that day when I shall meet Him face-to-face.

I pray that this revision of *The Spirit-Controlled Woman* will do the same for you. Let's begin by taking a look at what temperament is and then reviewing the various temperaments and how they influence our lives.

2

What Is Temperament?

*N*o examination of human beings is complete unless *temperament is considered, for it has more influence on their behavior than any other one* factor in life. Just as our physical, mental, and emotional makeup is based on the arrangement of genes at the time of conception, so is our temperament. It is well known that the combination of those genes produces the color of your eyes and hair, the shape of your skull and face, your height and general body shape, your IQ, and your emotional expression and responses. What is not so well known is that those same genes produce your temperament. They, in turn, have a significant influence on the way you use your physical, emotional, and mental traits.

Your temperament (or I should say, your unique combination of two or more temperaments), together with your physical, mental, and emotional characteristics, is what makes you uniquely you. Even identical twins will act differently because of their different temperament combinations, for temperament determines how you use your physical, mental, and emotional characteristics.

Nothing has a more powerful influence on human behavior than temperament. Of course, your spiritual nature can help strengthen your temperament's weaknesses, but we will discuss that later. For now, it is important to understand that your unique combination of temperaments determines your actions, reactions, prejudices, and often your likes and dislikes. Admittedly, other factors play a role in why you act the way you do, including your childhood training, religious values, habits, and education.

Some researchers say that a passive child in the womb will be passive in life, and that a kicker in the womb will be a kicker in life. I do know that it is often easy to predict the primary temperament of some children in a nursery. For example, the choleric child cannot stand to be placed in a crib when she does not want to sleep. You can almost see what she is thinking by the look in her eyes as she shakes the bars unmercifully ("As soon as I get out of this crib, I am going to organize this whole house!"). The phlegmatic child is content to while away his time playing with the toys he has been given. The melancholy child cries as if she has been abandoned for life—and she thinks she has been. The sanguine child turns on the charm every time someone walks by, hoping the person cannot resist and will pick her up—and usually she is right.

When you meet these people 25 years later, you will find that their basic temperament traits still characterize their behavior. The fun-loving sanguine is still a happy-go-lucky person; the hard-driving choleric is still trying to organize everything, though by this time his horizon has changed. Now he is organizing his own company or a whole city. The melancholy still knows that people don't like her and will abandon her if given a chance; and the phlegmatic is still content to putter around, though by now he will smell the roses and look at the flowers.

Someone has said of the four temperaments that the creative melancholy invents things, the choleric manufactures them, the sanguine sells them, and the phlegmatic enjoys them.

CAN TEMPERAMENT BE CHANGED?

Melancholies commonly ask, "Can my temperament be changed?" Sanguines rarely ask that question because they like themselves and like the fact that most other people like them too. Cholerics don't want to change, but they would like to change most other people. Phlegmatics are usually content to happily watch others as spectators in life. Ironically, the melancholy—the richest and most talented of all the temperaments—is the one most likely to want a different temperament It must be the perfectionist bent in the melancholy that is always looking for the right mix to make her "perfect." Once she realizes she is a member of the fallen race of Homo sapiens and that no one is perfect, she may be willing to accept herself and use her considerable gifts.

But the bottom line is, no, your temperament cannot be changed. Like your fingerprints, it is an identifying part of your being for life. Happy is the woman who understands that God made her the way she is and wants to use her that way.

He had a plan for you when you were conceived, and will use all your life circumstances to mold you into the person He wants you to be, if you allow Him to do so. Your weaknesses should make you realize your dependency on Him, and that is what this book is really all about. By understanding your weaknesses, you can overcome them through the filling of the Holy Spirit. God then can use your talents to the maximum degree.

Most people are so dominated by the weakness side of their temperament that they destroy their inherited strengths. Theologically, we would say that "the sin that so easily besets you" keeps you from fulfilling your mission in life. For example, the sanguine is often the victim of personal ego and lack of self-discipline. Later in life she often repels people instead of attracting them. The choleric so brutalizes people with her razor-sharp and sarcastic tongue that they are afraid of her. The phlegmatic often indulges her selfish spirit of not wanting to get involved or not wanting to push herself. And the melancholy can indulge her naturally pessimistic, moody self and make herself an emotional basket case who complains so much that people avoid her—just as she expected.

BUT SOME PEOPLE SEEM TO CHANGE!

Many people seem to change their temperament as they go through life. But if you look carefully, you will find it is only when some higher and external source of power comes into their life and strengthens their weakness that they experience that change. In some it is their love for another person. Some women who were abused and put down by a parent, marry men who are affirming and supportive. That support and encouragement provides the much-needed confidence that enables them to appear to change. But even then the change is limited to certain areas of their life.

ð

While no woman can change her temperament, the spiritual power available to her in the Holy Spirit can transform her basic weaknesses so much that she seems to change her temperament.

ð

Some women find alcohol, drugs, or another form of addictive behavior the temporary means of external support to lift them out of their weaknesses. But the harmful side effects are well known and often run their course, creating more problems in the long run than any woman can cope with.

The best and only external source of power for a woman today is the ministry of the Holy Spirit available to her after she becomes a Christian. There are no negative side effects to the spiritual change through the Holy Spirit, and it is not temporary. I will discuss that in more detail in another chapter. But right now I want to emphasize that, while no woman can change her temperament, the spiritual power available to her in the Holy Spirit can transform her basic weaknesses so much that she seems to change her temperament.

GOD DID NOT CHANGE
THE APOSTLES' TEMPERAMENTS

In his book *Transformed Temperaments*, my husband, Tim, used biblical characters as examples of the kind of "change" God can produce in any individual who accepts Him as Lord and Savior and allows Him to control his life. Peter was a superextrovert sanguine when Christ came into his life. After he was filled with the Holy Spirit in Acts 2, he did not cease being an extrovert. Instead, God was able to use his outgoing, contagious spirit to win thousands to his Lord. The apostle Paul was a strong-willed, hard-driving extrovert before he ever became a Christian. But after he was saved and filled with the Holy Spirit, he dedicated his talents to God and became what many consider the most productive Christian in the first century and, through his 13 epistles, maybe in the whole of Christianity. Likewise, Moses the melancholy and Abraham the phlegmatic were totally ineffective for God until they were empowered by the Spirit of God.

Because temperament is built into you at conception, temperament change is not possible. But changing your weaknesses is another story. As we will see, God the Holy Spirit will provide strength for every human (or temperament) weakness. The result will be what seems like a change. And isn't that what you want? Everyone would like to overcome his or her weaknesses. The only power I know that can do that is the Holy Spirit. But it is not automatic just because you are a Christian. Change will only come about when you cooperate with the Holy Spirit.

3

The Four Basic Temperaments

*W*hat could be more interesting than the study of human temperament? It is what unlocks the door to understanding why people act the way they do. Everyone, of course, is interested in what makes people tick. And as fascinated as we are in what makes other people behave the way they do, almost all of us are interested in the secret behind our own behavior.

Eighty percent of all college students take Psychology 101 and 102, probably because they are trying to find what causes their spontaneous actions and reactions. Almost everyone has asked, "Why do I do what I do?" or "Why do I act the way I do?" The trouble with humanistic psychology is that it basically divides people into only two categories: "introvert" and "extrovert." Unfortunately, that is much too inadequate an explanation of human behavior. The four basic temperaments are far more descriptive and make it easier for people to identify themselves.

Surprisingly, temperament is the oldest theory of human behavior. It is also the most accurate. Temperament theory was conceived by the Greek physician Hippocrates, who is known as the "father of modern medicine." He must have been an analytical genius, for the original characteristics he gave each temperament have survived for over 2000 years.

Although Hippocrates was not the first to see that there were four kinds of people, he was the first to identify the four types and give them names that have stuck for 23 centuries. Solomon, the wise man of Proverbs, saw four kinds of people 500 years before Dr. Hippocrates was born. And although Solomon did not identify the four types with the names we are familiar with, he described their negative characteristics as follows:

> There is a generation that curses its
>   father, And does not bless its mother.
> There is a generation that is pure in its
>   own eyes,
>   Yet is not washed from its filthiness.
> There is a generation—oh, how lofty are
>   their eyes!
>   And their eyelids are lifted up.
> There is a generation whose teeth are like
>   swords,
> And whose fangs are like knives,
> To devour the poor from off the earth,
> And the needy from among men.
>
> —Proverbs 30:11-14

I have found it interesting that Solomon, described in the Bible as "the wisest man that ever lived or that ever would live," listed the melancholy temperament first. In every listing from Hippocrates to the present, most writers on this subject have started with the sanguine. But I am going to follow Solomon's listing and introduce you to Martha Melancholy first. Before we proceed to that description, however, I want to give you the good news and the bad news about temperament.

> *I have found the four temperaments to not only be the best explanation of human behavior, but also the best tool for helping people cope with their weaknesses because Scripture has an answer for each of these weaknesses.*

All temperaments have strengths and weaknesses. And while I will describe both areas, we will examine the weaknesses of each temperament more carefully than the strengths. Our strengths do not cause us much trouble in life, since they usually provide our unique set of talents. Although more of us women would like to be known only by our strengths, unfortunately the weaknesses often are more obvious. Therefore, I am going to concentrate on the weaknesses of each temperament more than the strengths, because it is our weaknesses that cause us the most problems. If we can learn to rely on the ministry of the Holy Spirit who is in us after we receive Christ as our personal Savior and Lord, then we can go on to become the kinds of people God originally intended us to be.

I have found the four temperaments to not only be the best explanation of human behavior, but also the best tool for helping people cope with their weaknesses because Scripture has an answer for each of these weaknesses. Once we understand that we are not abnormal and that many other people share our particular traits, then there is hope for us with God's help. It will then be easier to begin the gradual process of overcoming our most detrimental weaknesses. But first we should understand the four temperaments, particularly as they relate to women.

We will consider the four temperaments in the following order:

> Introverts—
>> Melancholic
>> Phlegmatic
>
> Extroverts—
>> Choleric
>> Sanguine

As we study these, I pray that you will do so with an open mind and heart. Only then can the Holy Spirit do a work in our lives that will enable us to more effectively glorify Him.

4

Meet Martha Melancholy

*M*artha Melancholy usually possesses the richest of all the temperaments. She is generally quite gifted by nature, with a high IQ and a retentive mind that is constantly analyzing everything. She often achieves good grades in school, enjoying the complex studies of chemistry, mathematics, and other precise subjects. If she has talents in the field of music, she will have a deep appreciation for good music and possibly be able to play an instrument or sing. She is usually a good speller and a precise grammarian. She is the student that teachers love because she gets her work in on time, and it is usually the neatest work in the class.

Martha is an introvert and, depending on her background, childhood training, and past experiences, she may rarely volunteer her opinion, even though she almost always has one. She is very sensitive, which may be why she does well in the health-care field.

There her self-sacrificing nature enables her to minister effectively to others, if her natural introversion and fear do not inhibit her. Once she works through the early days of a new vocation and becomes comfortable in her work, she will do extremely well with her innovative mind and creativity.

ɞ ———————————————

Rarely will Martha Melancholy have a lazy bone in her body. Instead, she is so industrious that she feels guilty if she isn't working.

————————————————— ɞ

Martha usually doesn't have many friends because she is so internal and sometimes overly self-occupied. She almost never seeks new friendships, and she really prefers to be alone or at best with one or two others. Once she does acquire a friend, Martha is extremely loyal to them. That may be one reason she has so few friends. She tends to feel disloyal to her first friend if she finds another. If you have a melancholy friend, you will be blessed because you will have a friend for life, provided you don't betray her or grieve her very sensitive spirit. Be warned: You can offend her very easily without even thinking about it. Often Martha Melancholy is so sensitive that you can offend her just by the *way* you look at her (or, even worse, if you don't look at her)!

Rarely will Martha Melancholy have a lazy bone in her body. Instead, she is so industrious that she feels guilty if she isn't working. She is not the active, bustling, busy type like Clara Choleric, whom we will examine later, but is more like Martha, the sister of Lazarus in the Bible, and is always busy trying to make life easier for other people. Melancholy children are often considered to be "model children." They live for the approval of their parents, teachers, and peer group. These children usually need little correction; in fact, parents of melancholies should be very careful when correcting them, for they are easily devastated by disapproval. Since they usually grow up to marry extroverts, who often are needlessly brutal in their criticism, the melancholy can feel unloved, unappreciated, and insecure.

Self-discipline is another typical hallmark of melancholies. They are the most likely of the temperaments to follow directions, maintain a physical fitness regimen, and keep the commitment of their wedding vows. Unfortunately, they even tolerate spousal abuse and molestation, which amazes other temperament types. Rarely will you find an obese Martha unless her secondary temperament is sanguine. For as we will see, sanguines "live to eat," while melancholies "eat to live." Martha almost never eats unhealthy food. She knows the calories and fat grams of most foods and subconsciously rejects anything that does not contribute to her health. Unless emotionally distraught, Martha will not fluctuate more than ten pounds in her adult years. I have one melancholy friend who hasn't varied in dress size in 30 years, in spite of bearing five children.

One of Martha Melancholy's most obvious traits is her perfectionism. And frankly, I can't always say whether that is a blessing or a curse. If she is an artist, performer, or singer, she will work tirelessly to achieve her standard of perfection, which could reach higher than that of her teachers or parents. Then she plunges into a depressed state because she has not measured up to her own expectations. Melancholies are often unhappy with themselves and their performance, even though their peers or employers or customers may be extremely pleased with their creations. And while melancholics are often critical of other people, in fairness I should point out they are usually even more critical of themselves, which may be one reason they are often in an edgy mood. As a matter of fact, Hippocrates named them "melancholy" because he thought their melancholia or "black mood," which he found so prevalent, was caused by having too much black blood. And while most melancholies would love to blame their moodiness and depressive tendencies on their blood, glands, or chemistry, the truth is that depression and down moods can more often be traced to mental attitudes rather than physical causes.

Unfortunately, Martha's self-discipline doesn't always carry over into her emotional life. Even when told that she can think herself into a "funk" and in some cases a deep depression, she may still hang on to her self-pitying thoughts or self-criticism that spend her emotional energy and make her "tired all the time." In addition, Martha's creative abilities can take over. She can invent more reasons to feel sorry for herself than any other temperament and will imagine or exaggerate rejections, injuries, and insults. Unfortunately, a person cannot indulge in bad thoughts (for whatever cause) without experiencing bad feelings.

This may be why the middle-aged Marthas of the world often look like they are older than they really are, for their faces often reflect the bad moods of their heart.

The good news for Martha Melancholy is that God loves her and wants to save her and bring the "joy of the Lord" into her life. The three patterns she must seek God's help in overcoming are negativism, criticism (both of herself and others), and a natural tendency to gripe about everything, rather than giving thanks.

The best therapy for Martha Melancholy is to read Philippians every day for 30 days and learn what Paul admonishes—contentment with what she has and with who she is. While joy may be spontaneous to the sanguine, it is one of the first-named fruit of the Spirit (Galatians 5:22,23) and the best antidote to Martha Melancholy's blahs, mood swings, and depressions. Praise music also will help to turn her thoughts toward thankfulness.

It is quite common for the Martha Melancholies of this world to get the false notion that "there is no hope for me." That is only true if they do not know Jesus Christ personally and do not have access to His power through the ministry of the Holy Spirit. I find it interesting that, in the Bible, God sought more melancholy people to serve Him than any others. Some of the greatest prayer warriors, who were self-sacrificing and faithful servants of our Lord, had melancholy temperaments. Just ask yourself: What temperaments were Moses, Elijah, Samuel, John the Baptist, the apostle John, Paul, and Thomas? They were all melancholics. But like all of these men, to be all you can be in service for our Lord or as a person, you must cooperate with the Holy Spirit.

The following are some of the characteristics unique to Martha Melancholy, plus a perspective on how the weaknesses of this temperament can be modified when controlled by the Holy Spirit.

Strengths of Martha Melancholy's emotions—
  Loves music and art
  Rich, sensitive nature
  Analytical ability
  Emotionally responsive
  Deep, reflective thinker

Emotional weaknesses—
  Moody and gloomy
  Pessimistic, always looking for the negative
  Likes to suffer, acts as a martyr
  Hypochondriac
  Introspective to the point of being harmful
  Depressive
  Proud

The melancholy has deep, dark moods of gloom and depression and will take on a more happy, cheerful countenance with the help of the Holy Spirit. Her introspective nature can learn to step out on faith and look toward the future with bright optimism.

Strengths of Martha Melancholy's
relationship to others—
    Dependable friend
    Self-sacrificing friend
    Faithful and loyal friend
    Makes friends cautiously
    Deep feeling for friends

Weaknesses in her relationships—
    Critical of others and any
        imperfections
    Searches for perfection and judges
        everything according to her ideals
    Fearful of what others think of her
    Suspicious of others
    Can erupt into violent anger after
        prolonged animosity
    Often deeply hurt by others
    Will carry a grudge and be
        revengeful
    Dislikes those in opposition
    Hard to get along with

Through the Holy Spirit, Martha Melancholy can develop a loving spirit, thus causing her to be less critical and suspicious of others and much easier to get along with.

Strengths of Martha Melancholy's
activities—
    Strong perfectionist tendencies
    Likes detail and analytical work

Self-disciplined; finishes what she
   undertakes
Fitted for creative, intellectual work
Conscientious and thorough
Gifted; genius-prone
Knows her own limitations

Weaknesses in her actions—
   Indecisive
   Theoretical and impractical
   Tires easily
   Hesitant to start a new project
   Too much analysis; leads to
      discouragement
   Life work must demand the greatest
      in sacrifice, self-denial, and service
   Becomes moody over creations

She will become more outgoing and less self-centered through the Holy Spirit. Her pessimism will be counteracted by a thanksgiving spirit if she is obedient to the Lord and keeps her eyes on Him and not on herself.

Some of the occupations and hobbies of
Martha Melancholy—
   Artist
   Musician
   Seamstress
   Culinary Arts
   Accountant
   Beautician

Spectator at athletic events
Educator—usually in math, science,
   or English
Interior Decorator
Fashion Designer
Author
Crafts
Poet—either to write or to enjoy

The greatest needs of Martha Melancholy
for spiritual growth—

1. To overcome her critical spirit.

2. To be delivered from self-absorption.

3. To become occupied in loving service for others, thus forgetting herself.

4. To develop a thankful spirit.

5. To walk in the Spirit on a daily basis.

6. To develop the mental habit of thanksgiving living—"in everything give thanks; for this is the will of God in Christ Jesus for you" (1 Thessalonians 5:18).

Martha Melancholy has other lesser needs, but nothing will transform her life as greatly as changes in these six. As she yields to the Holy Spirit in these areas, God will use her to the maximum and she will like herself much better—and so will her loved ones.

SUMMARY

The self-sacrificing, thinking Martha Melancholy is probably the most gifted of all the temperaments. And yet, because of her self-centeredness, her critical spirit, and her gloom, she suffers more than any of the others and limits her ability to use her talents and gifts. It is only when her heart and mind are controlled by the Holy Spirit that the melancholy can forget herself and her critical spirit and become a genuine Christian who helps those around her with a tender and sensitive nature. She can develop a thanksgiving heart that will become a pattern of living for her. Only then will she find fulfillment, peace, and satisfaction in Christ.

Some time ago, I counseled a Martha Melancholy type who was very concerned about the future. Her husband was not the man she thought she had married. He was not sufficiently productive, not ambitious, not neat, not helpful around the house, not even sexy enough, and she felt that life had been unfair to her. She was experiencing deep moods of depression and had even contemplated ending her life.

After listening to her steady stream of problems, I pointed out that all of her statements had been critical of her husband and how he had not met up to her standards of him. I thought perhaps this fellow was a complete dud, but I finally sent her home with an assignment. For the next week she was to develop a list of only positive, good things she could find in his character. I told her that if she was having difficulty finding anything to put on her list, she might have to ask God for help. She came back the following week and said that for the first three days she had nothing to report. Finally, she asked God to help her to see if there was any good in this man. Her list then consisted of four things: 1) he was good to the children, 2) he was generous with his money, 3) he was respected at their church as a fine Bible teacher, and 4) he was faithful to her. Her critical spirit was ruining their marriage and her life. She confessed this as sin and asked God to help her to stop being so critical and to stop judging him by her own ideals and standards. One year passed before I heard from her again. And then it was because she wanted me to know how thankful she was for her husband! Although he still had some of the same faults, she discovered that he also had some very great strengths, and she thanked God for this man.

Martha Melancholy has such great potential! Because she is naturally a loyal friend, when Jesus Christ becomes her Lord and Savior and she is controlled by the Holy Spirit, there is no other temperament with a greater dedication and devotion to God.

5

Meet
Polly Phlegmatic

*P*olly *Phlegmatic is not just an introvert; she is a superintrovert. She has a gracious and calm spirit, works well under pressure, and has so little* natural anger that she may live her entire life and never "blow her top." All who know her admire her easygoing, never-get-upset, well-balanced temperament. She is the epitome of dependability, is almost never late, and never offends anyone. Polly has many friends—in part because she is such a great listener. Rarely does she break a confidence. Not only is she pleasant most of the time, but she is usually very diplomatic as well. She is a peacemaker as soon as she can walk and talk. Even in the nursery, she is the child who usually takes toys to crying children. Polly just doesn't like to see people unhappy. She is the easiest person to like over the span of a lifetime.

The children of Polly Phlegmatic are particularly blessed, for Polly usually has "the patience of a saint" and will drop whatever she is doing to attend to her preschooler. Her children are rarely starved for love and often grow up with a good self-image. Through their actions, phlegmatic moms usually convey their genuine love for their children. The daughter of a phlegmatic mom very often is taught the basic elements of homemaking and may be skilled at them even before reaching high school. You name it—cooking, sewing, mothering—Polly can do it all. Patient Polly Phlegmatic is a good teacher, at home or in elementary school.

In today's world of testy labor relations between workers and management, many company executives look for Polly Phlegmatic types to place in management positions because of their diplomatic and people-sensitive nature.

Professionally, Polly is best known for her quiet efficiency. She is both creative and organized. Someone once said, "Phlegmatics even have the dust on their desk organized." One of our sons showed strong phlegmatic tendencies as he was developing. When he was in high school he would never go to bed without stacking his loose change in neat piles according to size and value. The fact that he would put it in his pocket the next morning made no difference. Polly is like that. Her closet will be neat with everything on hangers, in proper order, and grouped by dresses, skirts, slips, blouses, suits, etc. I have even heard of one phlegmatic who arranged her clothes according to color as well (and, of course, they would all be positioned with the front of the clothes in the same direction).

Polly may not share Martha Melancholy's high intelligence, but neither does she share her high susceptibility to emotional self-destruction. Polly's sense of organization, calm consistency, and dependability get her to her goals eventually and enable her to do well on tests. She is usually also a good speller and a quick learner. One of Polly's most helpful traits is her practical outlook on life. She is the one temperament that enjoys the artistic traits of the melancholy and the practical traits of the choleric. And while she usually shuns leadership, she is a good leader when the job is thrust upon her. In fact, in today's world of testy labor relations between workers and management, many company executives look for Polly Phlegmatic types to place in management positions because of their diplomatic and people-sensitive nature. They rarely offend anyone. When Polly does assume leadership, it is usually because she has a plan to reach her goals. Others also enjoy working with her because she never attempts anything by chance. Polly's motto is: "Always plan ahead, and you can accomplish more with less activity." Her biggest management weakness (and often matrimonial weakness) is her discomfort with confrontation. Rather than confronting an employee or a mate, Polly Phlegmatic will permit inadequate behavior to go on much too long.

To Polly's good traits, you can add her sense of humor. She has a dry wit that can see something funny in most situations. She uses it to dissolve tense moments and spread peace. She does not tell a lot of jokes like the sanguine temperament, but just says funny things. It is usually her dry sense of humor that can crack others up into peals of laughter, while she never cracks a smile. Most stand-up comics who make up their own material are predominantly phlegmatic. The flip side of that gift is that Polly will usually turn her humor into an art form as a means of protecting herself from involvement. There is no one like Polly Phlegmatic who can refuse your best pitch to get her to commit to something, without even offending you.

Because of these two traits, rarely will you find a phlegmatic with emotional problems that demand counseling, unless caused by her mate or children. The reason is basically twofold. Polly Phlegmatic almost always diffuses anger with a soft answer, because it is her style to strive for peace. The other is her sense of humor. Outwardly, Polly looks at life, people, and events through humorous glasses, but inwardly she may be questioning why someone said what they did and what was the hidden meaning.

But as gracious, lovable, and enjoyable as Polly Phlegmatic is to be around, even she is not perfect. In fact, if not caught early, Polly's passive weaknesses will eventually catch up to her and cause her to become a source of irritation. Chief among those weaknesses is Polly's selfish disposition. All temperaments do have a problem with selfishness, for it is part of our fallen nature. But Polly is selfish, self-protective and, in some cases, stingy. Ask any waitress, and she will tell you that phlegmatics are the lightest tippers of all the temperaments. I know of one phlegmatic who is married to a very sociable, sanguine husband. He is a generous tipper, but his wife so objects to the size of his tips that she pauses at the table long enough to cut the amount in half.

And it isn't just money that Polly is selfish with. She also tends to protect her time, energy, and emotions. Polly sometimes has a difficult time learning to love others (except for her children and her husband). Sometimes even they are shortchanged of her love. She may not be aware of it, for Polly is very protective. Hurt her once, and you may never get another chance— she will protect herself the next time.

In addition, Polly can be stubborn. That may shock you when you think of your phlegmatic friends, and particularly so if you aren't close to them. Underneath that gracious go-along spirit usually lies a stubborn streak of steel on matters about which Polly cares deeply. Understand, however, that Polly is very diplomatic. This may be why Polly is not well known as being stubborn, for she will often use humor, diplomacy, and grace to get her own way. But be sure of this: If Polly wants her own way, she will get it. As children, phlegmatics will rarely defy their parents by saying, "I will not do that! You can't make me do it." That sounds more like the strong-willed choleric child. But Polly Phlegmatic as a child simply will not obey her mother's order if she doesn't want to do it. I have often said phlegmatic children won't do what they don't want to do and be nicer about it than anyone else. But be sure of this: If they don't want to do something, they won't. This can be a great source of irritation in a marriage. And since Polly is likely to marry a strong-willed choleric, it is not uncommon for them to experience a "push-pull marriage."

One of Polly's traits that limits her in every area of life is her tendency to be passive in nature. On one side she may be patient, but on the other she seems to have a lifetime battle with the law of inertia. The older and slower she gets, the more it becomes a losing battle. This can be irritating to a mate who might like to entertain frequently, for self-protective Polly will find several diplomatic reasons for not entertaining. As a child she can "putter around" and waste more time than any child in class. Homework can be an endless contest of wills. As teens, phlegmatics can drift off into fantasy faster and longer than anyone else, and never get their work done. And as adults, phlegmatics will overprotect themselves from getting involved. Throughout their lifetimes, the only thing phlegmatics will ever over-involve themselves in is avoiding getting overinvolved. In fact, the Polly Phlegmatics of this world need to understand that they are the one temperament that should try to take on more than they think they can do, because it helps to motivate them. When opportunities come, phlegmatics shouldn't reject or avoid them because "they take too much time and effort." Instead, they should decide if it is God's will and then take on the opportunity. Since they are not self-motivated by nature, phlegmatics should take on external forms of pressure in order to help them achieve more and, in the end, like themselves better.

Polly Phlegmatic also carries around a syndrome of fear, worry, and anxiety. That, combined with her passive nature, results in a strong possibility that Polly will never fulfill her potential. Even in her first Sunday school Christmas performance, Polly will reveal her basic fear tendency when she ends in tears or is mute while all the other children are singing. Unless conquered by the Holy Spirit and the Word of God, Polly's fears will dominate her life and she will never live the life of faith of a believer. It is not uncommon for the Pollys of the church, who otherwise can be very dedicated to God, to refuse all opportunities for Christian service. Polly makes a good nursery worker or primary teacher, but rarely will she take on any of the responsibilities of adult work.

I know something about this characteristic. For many years I restricted my teaching to the junior Sunday school department because I let my fears keep me from teaching an adult Bible class. As an early teenager, I was taught how to work with children and lead them to Christ. But as a pastor's wife, I would hide behind my husband and say that I was a children's worker and that my husband was the adult speaker in our family. It was a thrilling (and a somewhat scary) day for me when I threw away my shell of self-protection and abandoned myself to God to do whatever He chose. By faith He has led me one step at a time to an exciting way of life that I never dreamed possible when dominated by my fears. Today I am privileged to be the president of the nation's largest pro-family women's organization, where I am in constant contact with adult women and men. It has been a great blessing to

realize that the fearful young minister's wife of yes-
teryear has now been transformed by the ministry of
the Holy Spirit. If you had told me 25 years ago that
someday I would have my own daily radio talk show
with an audience of almost a million people, I would
have been the first to say "impossible" or "no way!"
But that is unbelief. I can now honestly say that, to the
glory of God, I have come this far by faith. And so can
you! God has something special for you to do.

The following are some of the characteristics that
are unique to Polly Phlegmatic and a list of how Polly's
weaknesses can be modified when controlled by the
Holy Spirit.

> Strengths of Polly Phlegmatic's
> emotions—
>> Calm and dependable
>> Good-natured and easy to get along
>> with
>> Cheerful and pleasant even if she
>> doesn't have much to say
>> Kindhearted
>> Peace-loving
> Emotional weaknesses—
>> Lacks confidence in self
>> Pessimistic and fearful; worrier
>> Rarely laughs aloud
>> Passive and indifferent
>> Compromising
>> Self-righteous

Through the Holy Spirit, her fearful, worrying
nature will be replaced with the self-confidence of the

Spirit-filled life, and her pessimism will gradually turn to optimism.

Strengths of Polly Phlegmatic's relationship to others—
- Pleasant to be with
- Has many friends
- Dry, witty sense of humor
- Softening and conciliating effect upon others
- Constant and faithful
- Diplomatic and a peacemaker
- Good listener
- Faithful friend
- Gives advice only when asked

Weaknesses in her relationships—
- Doesn't allow herself to get involved
- Selfish and stingy
- Studies people with indifference
- Unenthusiastic
- Stubborn
- Indifferent about others
- Teases others who annoy her
- Not very cordial
- Attitude of superiority

With the Holy Spirit, Polly will develop a new love for people and will desire to get involved with others. Her selfish and indifferent spirit will also change.

Strengths of Polly Phlegmatic's activities—
- Works well under pressure

Practical, easy way of working
Conservative
Neat and proficient
Plans her work before beginning
Stabilizing influence
Dependable worker

Weaknesses in her actions—
Calm, serene, uninvolved spectator
in life
Slow and lazy
Reluctant leader
Lack of motivation
Indecisive
Overprotects herself from
involvement
Discourages others
Opposes change of any kind

The Holy Spirit will help Polly to lose her slow tendencies and laziness. She will also develop a new motivation for productivity as she becomes involved and senses the needs of those about her.

Some of the occupations and hobbies of Polly Phlegmatic—
Homemaker
Parent
Bookkeeper
Counselor
Teacher—elementary
Crafts
Reluctant leader

Administrator
Seamstress
Secretary
Gourmet cook
Athletic spectator

The greatest needs of Polly Phlegmatic for spiritual growth—

1. To overcome her passivity.
2. To learn to give of herself to others.
3. To stop acting like a Christian and begin trusting God for everything.
4. To recognize her fearfulness as sin and give it over to God.
5. Walk day by day in the control of the Holy Spirit.
6. Replace her natural fears with faith in our living Lord, which will enable her to take on the projects she would otherwise quickly decline, thus limiting herself by unbelief.

SUMMARY

The complacent, peaceful Polly Phlegmatic is probably the easiest to be around because of her easygoing and well-balanced nature. But she usually holds everyone at arm's length and protects herself from getting too involved with people or work. Her greatest need is to recognize that her fear, which is not of God, definitely limits her effectiveness for Christ. She needs to treat her indolence as a sin; then, through Jesus

Christ, Polly will be able to give of herself to others. Polly is quite a capable person when she is willing to let go of herself and let God take control.

There are many Polly Phlegmatics in our group of friends across the country, but very few of them will ever seek help even when they recognize they have a problem. There is one Polly in particular that comes to my mind. She was just about as fearful and introverted as any phlegmatic I have ever known. On the surface her friends were never aware that she had this turmoil going on inside, for she presented herself to others as a very calm, self-confident, and capable person. But one day she seemed to come unglued and confessed to me that what she represented on the outside was not at all what was taking place on the inside. (Even phlegmatics have their breaking point.)

She confessed how fearful she was of other people and how inadequate she thought she was. When asked to serve on a board in the church, she refused with a flimsy excuse. And when other leadership and ministry opportunities arose, she repeatedly responded the same way. It was then that she began to realize that she was cheating herself of many opportunities to serve Christ by her fear and indifference. Her children and husband were all active in the ministry of their church, but she was the one on the outside—uninvolved, indifferent, and supernegative. Finally, this began to show in her mental attitude toward her family and the church until, on one particular day, this dear lady faced the reality that she was being left in the dust spiritually. Her husband and children were outgrowing her spiritually as a result of her fear and selfishness. I read 2 Timothy 1:7 to her from my Bible:

"For God has not given us a spirit of fear, but of power and of love and of a sound mind." She then genuinely confessed her sin to Christ and prayed to be filled with the Holy Spirit, asking God to do a beautiful thing in her life. She desired not just to be involved in the ministry of her church, but also to be a warm, loving, motivated, godly woman who was freed from the fears that bound her within.

I have watched this Polly turn from a woman paralyzed by her own fears to a beautiful example of the Spirit-filled woman. Her husband and children are pleased and proud of the new lady at their house. It has been like watching a rosebud open into full maturity as a beautiful, sweet-smelling flower, bringing joy and leaving a fragrance with all those who come in contact with her.

6

Meet Clara Choleric

*C*lara Choleric is definitely an extrovert with a dynamic personality. She is a natural-born leader and rarely hesitates to tell others what to do—whether she is qualified to do so or not. She never lacks something to do. If her environment doesn't provide enough activity, her busy mind will think of more than enough to occupy her 24 hours a day.

One of my daughters is predominantly a choleric. I didn't know anything about temperament when she was four years old, but I recognized that she was a born leader. Upon listening to her at play where she was busy ordering her friends around, I witnessed her "teaching school." What was interesting was that the three boys she was teaching were in kindergarten and first grade, but she had taken charge as teacher and was telling them all just what to do—and she was only four and had never been to school. Leadership techniques can be taught, as we have seen, for phlegmatics can learn to be leaders. But cholerics are born that way.

Clara loves activity. Her friends often think of her as a perpetual motion machine. Many marvel at all she gets done and wonder aloud where she gets all her energy. Her environment may stimulate her, but she is not dependent on it, since she usually stimulates her environment. Clara is extremely goal-oriented, which may account for her boundless energy. Her busy mind can always find something for her to do, and most of it is meaningful. By nature she is practical, and has little appreciation for music, art, or the aesthetic things of life. She would rather organize a concert as a means of raising money for her favorite organization than attend one.

Speaking of determination, Clara Choleric has it to burn. That is why she is usually so successful in life (in everything but interpersonal relationships).

Some cholerics have learned to become musicians, but you can credit their skill to an equally choleric parent who made them spend hours practicing their instrument. And when they play, their music lacks emotion and is more mechanical. Our church once interviewed a couple for the minister of music's position. The wife played the piano for our evening service and was flawless (but, I might add, expressionless).

What feeling she did portray in her style was created by her melancholy husband who arranged or wrote all of her music, even though he had never had a piano lesson. But he had that "feel" for music that is all but impossible to acquire, or else this Clara would have had it by sheer determination.

Speaking of determination, Clara Choleric has it to burn. That is why she is usually so successful in life (in everything but interpersonal relationships). She will make up her mind to do something, and she does it. Woe to the man or woman who gets in her way! President Clinton's wife, Hillary, is a typical example of a determined, goal-oriented Clara Choleric. Her example was clear when she made up her mind that she was going to develop a universal health-care program for all Americans. Ultimately, her method of planning this radical project was challenged in the courts, and her program fell under its own weight. But she was not destroyed. Being a choleric, Hillary Clinton picked herself up and went on to aggressively take on a new project.

Clara Choleric can use feminine charm to get her way if it serves her purpose, particularly if her secondary temperament is sanguine or melancholy. As we will see, sanguines are charmers and melancholies are actors. Although charm is not Clara's thing, if the situation demands it, she can act the part as long she is on the stage. Once she returns to the real world, her natural traits kick in and she loses that assumed charm. Some Claras can even be cruel, cutting, and abusive of others.

Cholerics are often considered smarter than they really are. This is due to their active brain that is always thinking and is invariably practical. Cholerics lack the genius of the melancholy creative inventor, but they possess the organizational skills of the productive manufacturer. In the business world you will usually find cholerics at the highest pay scale or as the owners of their own business. In my work, I am frequently positioned opposite choleric feminists when opposing many of the anti-family excesses of the feminist movement. In fact, most of the leaders of that anti-family movement are strong-willed cholerics who don't have a high regard for men or anyone else who opposes them. Unless they have a very passive husband, women like that often have a hard time maintaining a good marriage. Choleric wives often struggle with the biblical role of submission. And most men cannot stand to be dominated by a woman in the home, which produces its own long list of emotional and personality conflicts. There can only be one head of a family without marital disharmony resulting. And that head should be the husband, not only for the sake of the marriage, but also for the children. Many Spirit-filled Clara Cholerics have learned wifely submission out of obedience to the Lord and now enjoy the undying love of their husband and children. But if she is a strong choleric (such as a 60 to 75 percent blend of choleric), it is never easy. Abraham's wife, Sarah, provided a good example of that struggle in the Bible.

Most women prefer a strong, loving leader in the home because their basic natural tendencies are toward mothering, nurturing, and encouraging. And the older a woman gets, the more she wants to lean on her husband for both financial and emotional support. Unfortunately, if a woman begins by dominating him in the early days of her marriage, she either drives him out of her life and is left to a life of singleness, or she creates a weak man whom she ultimately does not respect or like. This is not a pretty picture for even a strong choleric.

As a pastor's wife, I have noticed that the Clara Cholerics of the congregation can be either a great blessing or a real source of trouble in the church. No one can get things done faster than Clara, which is why she inevitably is elected chairman of whatever board on which she sits. If she uses that position as a source of power to dominate the pastor as she does her husband, it will cause real trouble, and of course is not biblically correct. If the pastor is a good man but a weak leader, Clara can run all over him and will try to manipulate the entire church to do her will—after all, she knows her ways are best for everyone. But if Clara's pastor is a strong leader, he will be forced to do battle with Clara, which can lead to a divisive atmosphere. Like all other temperaments, Clara must be filled with the Spirit to be of use to God. Some godly choleric women have put their talents to action as Bible teachers for adult women. In that direction the Spirit of God and His Word has access to her heart, mind, and conscience, and that can have a revolutionary effect on her life.

The Claras of the world are extremely outspoken, opinionated, strong-willed, and fearless. This is a problem for cholerics that the other two more introverted temperaments do not have, and it becomes apparent whenever they are not controlled by the Holy Spirit. Their mouth usually gives them away. It also adds to their natural anger problem, which causes them to overtly express themselves.

My husband, Tim, and I saw an interesting example of a Clara Choleric in one of our congregations. We had only been in our new church about a year or so before we noticed that everyone in the church was afraid to cross Clara Choleric. She had run over every minister before my husband (who is a choleric-sanguine) and was soon running head-on into him. Fortunately for us and the church, Tim was preaching a series of messages on the Spirit-filled life and was trying desperately for the first time in his life to live that way. But then here was a woman who had intimidated everyone to elect her to positions on boards where she could run the church.

As Tim preached on the characteristics of a godly, Spirit-filled woman, she obviously fell far short. She had left too many dead bodies or walking wounded in that congregation to ever be described as being filled with love, joy, or peace. When she didn't get her way she would stomp her feet and, as she would say, "give them a piece of my mind." It didn't take the congregation long to realize that this strong-willed, angry, hardworking, capable woman was not a spiritual woman. She was selfish, hostile, and carnally determined to have her own way. Before long everyone had grown tired of her and she was placed on the shelf, which she found intolerable. Eventually she even tried to walk in the Spirit, but at best it was an on-again, off-again effort for years. For while she believed in the Spirit-filled life, as is typical of many cholerics, she thought it was for other people.

Many churches have, however, benefited greatly from some very capable cholerics. But I fear that many Clara Cholerics have gone down the drain of self-will and the determination to "do it my way." It is possible, though, for Clara Choleric to walk in the Spirit and be totally transformed. If you doubt that, study the life of the choleric apostle Paul. To be used of God, Clara Cholerics must do two things:

1. Walk in the Spirit and seek to do God's will and not theirs day by day.

2. Gain victory over their lifetime battle with the harmful emotion of anger and replace it with love, joy, and peace from the Holy Spirit.

The following are some of the characteristics unique to Clara Choleric and how the weaknesses of this temperament can be modified when controlled by the Holy Spirit.

Strengths of Clara Choleric's emotions—
Confident and a natural leader
Strong-willed and self-determined
Optimistic
Self-sufficient
Fearless and bold

Emotional weaknesses—
Violent anger problem
Highly opinionated
Insensitive to needs of others

Unemotional and cold
Little appreciation for aesthetics
Unsympathetic and harsh
Impetuous and violent
Disgusted by tears

Clara Choleric's worst enemy is her violent anger problem. But she can expect the Holy Spirit to help her get this under control as she commits it to God.

Strengths of Clara Choleric's relationships—
Does not expect anyone else to do something she can't do
Not easily discouraged
Strong leader
Good judge of people
Motivator
Exhorter
Never daunted by circumstances

Weaknesses in her relationships—
Lack of compassion
Makes decisions for others
Cruel, blunt, and sarcastic
Tends to dominate a group
Arrogant and bossy
Uses people for own benefit
Unforgiving and revengeful
Prone to bigotry
Haughty and domineering

The Holy Spirit will give Clara a compassionate heart and enable her to become more forgiving and thoughtful, less sarcastic and bossy, and willing to listen to the concerns of other people.

Strengths of Clara Choleric's activities—
    Good organizer and promoter
    Decisive; intuitive ability to make
        decisions
    Quick and bold in emergencies
    Keen, quick mind
    Great capacity for action
    Does not vacillate
    Very practical
    Stimulates others to activity
    Thrives on opposition
    Sets goals and reaches them

Weaknesses in her actions—
    Overly self-confident
    Crafty
    Prejudiced
    Opinionated
    Bored by details
    Nonanalytical
    Forces others to agree to her plan
    Tiresome and hard to please
    Allows time only for her own plans
        or projects

Through the Holy Spirit, Clara Choleric will seek to be open-minded and less opinionated. The realization will come to her that other people tend to have some very good ideas also, and she can put her efforts behind accomplishing their projects.

Some of the occupations and hobbies of Clara Choleric—
Strong leader
Professional career
President of women's work
Home entertainer
Executive secretary
Participant in athletics
President of local P.T.A.
Administrator
High school teacher
Precinct worker
Bank trust officer
Crusader
Political activist

The greatest needs of Clara Choleric for spiritual growth—
1. To become sensitive to the needs of others.
2. To confess her angry and cruel spirit.
3. To develop her inner beauty by quiet hours spent reading the Bible and praying.

SUMMARY

The lively, energetic Clara Choleric can outproduce all the other temperaments put together. However, to reach her goals she probably has offended and run over the feelings of other milder temperaments that may have stood in her way. When she allows the Holy Spirit to soften her insensitivity to other people and learns to love with a compassionate heart, Clara Choleric can be a mighty crusader for the cause of Jesus Christ.

▪ ▪ ▪ ▪ ▪

A very upset Clara Choleric stood before me one night pouring out her broken heart. When Clara Choleric gets to this place, she has had to go through a very traumatic experience which she cannot control or manipulate. This Clara was frustrated, angry, and broken and had finally come to me for help.

I had just finished speaking that evening at the first session of a weekend women's retreat. The four basic temperaments had been presented with their strengths and weaknesses. As I unfolded the story of cholerics, I pointed out that they are untiring drivers, who usually dominate and make decisions for everyone around them. In addition, I noted how they are often hostile and cruel women. The Holy Spirit seemed to use this description of the choleric to reach this Clara's heart. She was all of these and more. Through her hot tears, she told me the story of her 15-year-old son who had finally had all of this angry woman he could take and had run away from home. She had bossed her husband around and tried to dominate him, and he had finally turned to alcohol. The pastor of her church had even tried to help her earlier in her life, but she became angry at him and refused his help.

Clara had blown up and told the congregation off and was now left without many friends. In fact, she said that her relatives did not like to spend holidays with her because she usually had an explosion of anger before the day was over. This dear lady had finally come to the end of her rope and was able to hear the Holy Spirit speaking to her about her miserable condition.

Together we prayed as she asked forgiveness for her sinful wretchedness and then asked to be filled with and controlled by the Holy Spirit. She prayed especially that she might learn to give love, to like people, and to control her violent temper. I wish I could report that after praying this prayer for forgiveness her husband immediately stopped his drinking and her son came home. But I am sorry to say that Clara had to bear the scars she made on the other members of her family. She can only trust God to change her so completely that her family will see the transformation in her life and be willing to change. If only Clara had made this decision earlier in her life, or had allowed her minister to help her many years ago, she could have been saved from the heartaches caused by her anger.

7

Meet Sarah Sanguine

S *arah Sanguine is the superextrovert temperament with a fun-loving personality who is always the life of the party. She has a warm and happy disposition that* is contagious. Sarah is also the one with charisma to burn and the natural ability to lift the spirit of others, often motivating them to new heights of success, happiness, and fulfillment. Sarah may have been a cheerleader in high school, and she goes through life seeking to lift the spirits of others and bring joy into their lives. She is a natural saleswoman and a fascinating storyteller.

The moment Sarah enters the room, she begins lifting the spirit of others. You can't have a party without her, for she makes people laugh with her endless chatter and list of jokes and funny experiences. She loves people and enjoys talking; it has been said more than once that a sanguine enters the room mouth first. But she is easily the friendliest person you will meet and has an amazing ability to melt even the coldest personality. Melancholies usually resist a sanguine's cheerful spirit at first as "unrealistic," but even they begin looking forward to her fellowship. As one melancholy said, "I feel so good around Sarah Sanguine.

Sarah Sanguine is in the good humor business. She spreads good humor and cheer wherever she goes. She rarely meets a stranger, for within 30 seconds a stranger feels like a long-lost friend.

She helps me get my mind off all my troubles." Perhaps that is why melancholies often marry sanguines. They are the one person who makes melancholies feel good. But after marriage, melancholies can often be driven to irritation and distraction when their sanguine spouses reveal disastrously disorganized and undisciplined ways.

Sarah Sanguine is in the good humor business. She spreads good humor and cheer wherever she goes. She rarely meets a stranger, for within 30 seconds a stranger feels like a long-lost friend. She also does not wait for other, less free-spirited individuals to start a conversation, for Sarah can always be counted on to open the conversational door. On elevators it is Sarah Sanguine who speaks first, putting others at ease. She considers group silence a challenge to get other people talking. But Sarah Sanguine has to be careful that her open friendliness isn't taken as being flirtatious. Unfortunately, she has to learn early in life that an innocent greeting can be misconstrued as a come-on.

Sarah is never at a loss for words, though some of her spontaneous chatter can become rather inane. The biblical phrase "your speech betrays you" is certainly true of Sarah, who is not a deep thinker; consequently, her conversation gives her away. No other temperament goes away from a party or gathering like Sarah Sanguine, wishing she had said less and listened more. She convinces herself that "everyone knows how shallow I really am." And she means it. She will commit to "keeping my big mouth shut" the next time and she does (until she meets people, and then away she goes, talking a mile a minute). It's almost as if the sight of people opens Sarah's mouth.

The emotional side of Sarah's life is always right at the surface. She can cry at the drop of a hat. And it doesn't take much to bring on those tears: a news story, laundry tickets, or birds flying overhead. The good side of this is that Sarah shows compassion for others easily. The bad side it that Sarah lacks emotional control (although, in fairness to Sarah, she can often laugh as easily as she cries—sometimes for no reason, and sometimes much too loudly). It is this easy swing of emotion that often gives people the impression that Sarah is emotionally insincere. The truth is, Sarah is just emotionally expressive.

One result of this emotional responsiveness is that Sarah can be swept off her feet quickly in matters of the heart. With her strong desire to please other people, Sarah can easily be led into sexual temptation unless

her moral values are deeply rooted in a strong character. On the other hand, she does not dwell on the
tragedies of life. Sarah is capable of forgetting the
unhappy present and will set out to pursue a happier
future (that she somehow always knows is just around
the corner).

As lovable and expressive as Sarah is, she also has
more than her share of weaknesses, chief of which is
her weak will. Sarah's lack of discipline, unless for-
tified by the Spirit-filled life, is usually reflected in
every area of her life. She loves rich food, and it shows.
Many sanguines are 30 pounds overweight by the
time they are 30 years of age, and can expect to gain
another 3 to 5 pounds a year unless they face their
weight problem and develop a disciplined program to
overcome it. But it isn't just Sarah's weight that shows
her weakness. Her lack of self-discipline also often
results in a habit of talking too much, failing to establish good work patterns, and giving in to her emotional
excesses.

For Sarah Sanguine, anger is a special problem.
Because she is so verbal, consequently Sarah is often
known for her "angry explosions." In fairness, Sarah
repents easily for her angry outbursts and apologizes.
Everyone usually succumbs to her charm and then
forgives her. But after a while, that pattern gets pretty
old. Sarah not only apologizes easily, but she also doesn't
usually carry a grudge. Once she erupts, she forgets
all about it. You may not forget, but she does. That's
probably why sanguines don't have much trouble
with bleeding ulcers—they give them to everyone
else! By contrast, Clara Choleric, who can get mad
almost as fast as Sarah Sanguine, doesn't forget after

she erupts. Clara can continue to explode many times for the same insult, injury, or rejection—but not Sarah Sanguine. Once her anger is expressed, Sarah is ready to tackle her next crisis.

And Sarah usually lives from crisis to crisis. This is due to her lack of self-discipline, her inability to plan ahead, and her habit of agreeing to do more than her schedule could possibly allow her to do. Sarah Sanguine is so spontaneous by nature that she finds it difficult to engage in long-range planning. Consequently, her life is filled with endless disastrous experiences that have been brought on by her disorganization. Perhaps that is why tardiness, not paying bills on time, or not keeping well-intentioned commitments clutter Sarah's life with unnecessary pressures. And it may be one reason that, even though she was voted "most likely to succeed" in college, Sarah often fails to reach her full potential in life.

Sarah is famous for procrastinating. The challenge of doing the next activity dulls her motivation to finish her initial task and follow through on her assignments or commitments. Most sanguines would rather sit around with people and talk about work than engage in it. Sarah needs to set reasonable self-discipline standards for herself and keep them. She also needs to finish the present task before taking on the next. Sanguines are not lazy by nature, but they do tend to engage in much meaningless and unproductive activity.

Sarah Sanguine also needs to develop sales resistance. The old saying is true that "the easiest person to sell a product to is a good salesperson." As such, sanguines have no sales resistance. Consequently, they are often heavily in debt. The good news is there is much hope for Sarah Sanguine in the ministry of the Holy Spirit. The apostle Peter would have been known as the likable, charming buffoon of church history if he had not had an encounter with our Lord and the Holy Spirit—an encounter that transformed his life. And that power is available to any temperament today.

The two things most needed by Sarah Sanguine are to . . .

1. Seek to walk in the Spirit on a day-by-day basis to bring discipline, order, and purposeful living into her life.

2. Gain victory and control over her volatile emotions, particularly her outbursts of anger.

The following are some of the characteristics unique to Sarah Sanguine and how the weaknesses of this temperament can be modified when controlled by the Holy Spirit.

Strengths of Sarah Sanguine's emotions—
> Warm and lively
> Charismatic
> Talkative—never at a loss for words
> Carefree—never worries about the future or frets about the past
> Compassionate toward others

Great storyteller
Lives in present
Infectious conversationalist
Unusual capacity for enjoyment

Emotional weaknesses—
Cries easily
Emotionally unpredictable
Restless
Spontaneous outbursts of anger
Exaggerates the truth
Appears phony
Lacks self-control
Emotional decisions; impulsive buyer
Naive and childlike
Comes on too strong

Sarah Sanguine is a very emotional gal. She is never very far from tears and is usually emotionally unstable. However, the Holy Spirit can stabilize her emotions and calm her restless spirit. With God's help she can develop self-control and a disciplined life.

Strengths of Sarah Sanguine's relationships—
Makes friends easily
Responsive to people
Enjoyable and optimistic
Always friendly and smiling
Apologizes easily
Tender and sympathetic
Converses with genuine warmth

Shares other people's joys and
sorrows

Weaknesses in her relationships—
Dominates conversation
Not attentive
Weak-willed and has little conviction
Seeks credit and approval
Enjoys people and then forgets them
Makes excuses for negligence
Talks too often about herself
Forgets promises and obligations

Sarah will become a genuine friend and show more interest and concern with the lives of other people than the other temperaments. Her attention on herself will have to be minimized to be a Spirit-filled sanguine.

Strengths of Sarah Sanguine's activities—
Makes good first impression
Not bored because she lives in the
present
Gifted in caring for the sick
Easily engages in new plans or
projects
Breeds enthusiasm

Weaknesses in her actions—
Completely disorganized
Undependable; late
Undisciplined

> Wastes time talking when should be
>   working
> Many unfinished projects
> Easily distracted
> Falls short of goal

Unfinished projects and disorganization should become a thing of the past as she matures in her Christian life. With the help of the Holy Spirit, Sarah Sanguine will certainly become a more productive person.

> Some of the occupations and hobbies of
> Sarah Sanguine—
>   Actress
>   Women's speaker
>   Saleswoman
>   Visiting and caring for the sick
>   Good cook
>   Volunteer work
>   Counselor at a crisis pregnancy
>   center
>   Loving mother
>   Foster home parent
>   Leader
>   Given to hospitality
>   Receptionist
>   Participant in athletics

> The greatest needs of Sarah Sanguine for
> spiritual growth—
>   1. To be more reliable and
>   dependable.

2. To develop a greater self-disciplined life.
3. To replace her ego with genuine humility.

SUMMARY

The warm-hearted, loquacious Sarah Sanguine is the most outgoing of all the temperaments. She has the unique ability to enjoy each moment as it comes. This causes her many problems, however, because while enjoying this moment, Sarah usually forgets what she promised in the previous moments. The Holy Spirit will help her to become more dependable and faithful when she recognizes her need and asks God for help in this area. Sarah has the potential of being a delightful and productive Christian when she becomes self-disciplined and lets the Holy Spirit control her life.

Although Sarah is the most fun-loving and outgoing temperament, she suffers a great deal because of her noisy manner, self-indulgence, and weak will. I saw this vividly portrayed in the life of a typical Sarah Sanguine. This gal was a friendly, outgoing person, but her loud laughter and noisy remarks caused many of her friends to keep their distance. It was true to say she usually entered a room with her mouth first. Her excessive talking and high-pitched laughter were extremely aggravating to her melancholic husband. As a result, he was constantly trying to get her to be a quieter person like himself. But this caused Sarah a great deal of frustration because she was not a naturally quiet person. So she began to take her frustrations out by eating between meals and before bedtime, which resulted in a rapid increase in her weight. And because she suffered from a weak will and self-indulgence problem, the constant eating became uncontrollable. I watched Sarah put on 20 or 30 pounds in a short time. This additional problem only disgusted her melancholic husband with her lack of self-control. Little did he realize that he had been the initiator of the situation.

Finally, in desperation she came to me asking what she should do. I first suggested that she and her husband read my husband's book *The Spirit-Controlled Temperament* and learn the strengths and weaknesses of each of their temperaments. I felt it was necessary for the husband to understand that a sanguine could never be as quiet as a melancholic. Then Sarah had to face her own individual problem and realize that her lack of self-control could be improved by the filling of the Holy Spirit. She needed to learn temperance, gentleness, peace, and faith. Her prayer was a very simple, genuine petition asking for divine help not only with her weight problem, but also with her loud, blustering laughter. She asked to be filled with the Holy Spirit and to experience the fruit of the Spirit as a result.

Sarah's problems did not change overnight. It was necessary for her to daily commit herself to God for help in these areas. During this time her husband, too, was gaining a new understanding and admiration for the strengths Sarah Sanguine has to offer. He began to realize what joy and cheer his sanguine wife had brought into his dark, dreary life.

Sarah has gradually trimmed off the extra pounds she had gained, and her noisy, blustering sounds seems to have changed to cheerful, happy, contented laughter that is both pleasing and contagious. The two of them are a beautiful example of how opposites can complement one another when controlled by the Holy Spirit. For without the Holy Spirit, opposites can produce great friction that will endure throughout their lifetime.

8

Which Temperament Are You?

*B*efore we take a look at temperament blends, let's pause to examine which temperament you are. In fact, even before you know more about the theory, it is good to diagnose your own basic or predominant temperament. For the more you know about the differences in temperament, the more prone you are to score yourself on a test as you would like to be, not as you really are. As in all self testing, the accuracy of the test is dependent on how honest or objective you are about yourself.

Keep in mind that you are not going to be 100 percent one temperament. That is what makes each of us so uniquely different.

Assuming your objectivity, it is not difficult to diagnose which of the four basic temperaments you are. Keep in mind that you are not going to be 100 percent one temperament. That is what makes each of us so uniquely different. As you will see, picking out your secondary temperament is more difficult. But since 60 percent or more of your behavior is caused by your primary temperament, we will begin by determining it first in the following simple test.

First, determine whether you are an introvert or an extrovert, which is really quite simple. Answer the following questions "yes" or "no":

1. In a group do you find it easy to enter into the discussion?

2. Are you a spontaneous quick-talker?

3. Do you consider yourself an active person (as opposed to a more deliberative person)?

4. When you get angry, do you "explode" verbally?

5. Does leadership come easily to you?

If you scored at least four of the above "yes," you are probably an extrovert, which means your primary temperament is either a sanguine or a choleric. If "no," you are probably an introvert, which suggests you are probably a melancholy or a phlegmatic.

For Extroverts Only—please answer "yes" or "no":

1. Do your friends think of you as "the life of the party"?

2. Is it easy for you to make friends?

3. Are you basically a happy, carefree person?

4. If you explode in anger, is it easy to forget about it later, or are you likely to carry a grudge?

5. Do you find it easy to apologize when you are wrong or offend someone?

6. Do you find it difficult to finish a task or project before taking on a new project?

7. Do you enjoy being with people rather than being alone?

8. Do you like to please other people?

9. Are you moved to tears easily by the heartaches of others?

10. Do you have a real problem with self-discipline, particularly in the area of weight control and handling details?

If you answered "yes" to at least seven of these questions, you are probably a predominantly sanguine person. If you answered "no" to at least seven, you are probably a choleric. If equally divided, you are probably a blend of both temperaments (a sanguine/ choleric combination) and it would probably take a more detailed temperament test to diagnose exactly which predominates.

For Introverts Only—please answer "yes" or "no":

1. Do you have strong perfectionist tendencies?

2. Do you see life as serious most of the time?

3. Do you get discouraged if your work or that of other people does not measure up to your standards?

4. Do you get annoyed at those who disagree with you?

5. Do you resent correction?

6. If insulted, rejected, or injured, do you tend to mull it over and occasionally lash out or explode?

7. Do you ever have feelings of depression or experience black moods?

8. Do you prefer being alone in contrast to being with people?

9. Do you often feel that generally people do not understand or do not like you?

10. Do you prefer to have a project going or something to do as opposed to having nothing to do?

If you answered "yes" to seven or more of these questions, you are probably predominantly a melancholy. If "no," you are predominantly a phlegmatic temperament. If evenly balanced, you are probably a combination of the two. If however, almost none of the questions apply fully to you, you are probably a strong melancholy temperament for they usually find it painful to answer "yes" to anything that isn't 100 percent true.

THE LaHAYE TEMPERAMENT ANALYSIS

Obviously this simple test is not adequate to fully evaluate your temperament. But it should give you an indication of which is your predominant temperament.

If you desire a more thorough test, I suggest you utilize the $10 discount certificate in the back of this book and order my husband's "LaHaye Temperament Analysis." It will give you a detailed, personalized, in-depth analysis of both your primary and secondary temperaments, your strengths and weaknesses, and your spiritual gifts. It will also provide vocational aptitudes and offer positive biblically based suggestions on how to overcome the weaknesses of your particular combination of temperaments. It is extremely accurate, beautifully bound, and will be a keepsake analysis of you that will last a lifetime.

9

The 12 Blends of Temperament

*T*hrough their genes, your parents and your four grandparents contributed to your physical, mental, and temperamental makeup at the time of your conception. Frequently, it is easy to see that physically. In fact, we recently saw a little boy who bore no resemblance to either of his parents but had many of the grandfather's traits. So it is with temperament. A person may bear more resemblance to a grandparent's temperament than to that of a parent.

That may be why many people don't see themselves in one single temperament, but identify better with two or, in some cases, three. With at least six people contributing to their makeup through the gene pool, and given the mixture of nationalities today, most people tend to be a combination of temperaments rather than a single temperament. Perhaps in ancient days when the four-temperament theory was first conceived and there were fewer cross marriages among the nationalities, it would have been easier to identify a person as 100 percent choleric or melancholy, etc. But today few people are born of two parents with exactly the same nationality. And even if they are, there are still a variety of temperaments within nationalities. For example, Germans are well known for being choleric or melancholy or both. Italians are usually expressive sanguines or melancholies, or both. Britons tend to be choleric, phlegmatic, or both, while Scots tend to be sanguine or choleric, or both. Consequently, your temperament combination may be as varied as your nationality mixture.

However, if you study the subject carefully and examine yourself objectively, you will usually be able to identify yourself in two temperaments of differing intensities (and, in a few cases, three). One will be the predominant temperament, the other secondary. What makes this complicated is that the amount of your primary temperament or its intensity varies. For example, your primary temperament may be 60 percent, and your secondary 40 percent. If you are a sanguine-phlegmatic, which we call a SanPhleg, the 60 percent sanguine would mean that you are an extrovert, but not nearly as expressive as a 60/40 percent sanguine-choleric. Compare these temperaments to water. If you pour a sanguine's very hot water (60 percent) into a phlegmatic's cool water (40 percent), you will end up with warm water. But if you pour a sanguine's very hot water (60 percent) into a choleric's hot water (40 percent), the end result will burn you. So it is with temperament combinations. Then add to that the further complication that the mixtures vary. A person could be 70 percent sanguine or even 80 percent, with the balance made up of one or more temperaments. Such people can easily identify their primary temperament but never be able to accurately pick out their secondary temperament.

৵ ————————————————————

Unless you are extremely strong in one temperament, your secondary temperament will have a significant influence on your behavior. It will either offset some of the weaknesses of your primary temperament or it will intensify them.

———————————————— ৵

In the LaHaye Temperament Analysis I referred to earlier, only 13 people have complained about the accuracy of their primary temperament diagnosis, and that test has been taken by well over 30,000 people! A larger group has trouble accepting the accuracy of secondary temperaments.

Unless you are extremely strong in one temperament, your secondary temperament will have a significant influence on your behavior. It will either offset some of the weaknesses of your primary temperament or it will intensify them. For example, both cholerics and melancholies have a problem with criticizing others. But that problem can be offset if mixed with a phlegmatic or sanguine temperament. But if the two are put together as a ChlorMel, or MelChlor, the problem will only be intensified. While it is true that some of their gifts will also be intensified, if that ChlorMel or MelChlor does not gain victory over her weaknesses, she will often never fully realize her potential.

Therefore, no study of temperaments is complete unless we examine the 12 combinations of temperaments which most people call "blends" of temperament. For that reason, I would like to briefly introduce you to my 12 friends that illustrate the blends of temperament. You will probably find that you identify with one of them more readily than you did in the basic four temperaments.

MEET MILLY MELSAN

One of the most gifted of all the temperament blends is Milly MelSan. She usually does well in academia, receiving A's and B's all through school. Although she is generally considered an introvert, she has enough sanguine to put some zest into her personality. She is often very good at music and can get so emotionally involved as a performer that she can sway an audience with her charm. When Shakespeare said, "All the world's a stage," he must have had MelSans in mind (or their reverse, the SanMel), for the melancholy side of her is given to acting even to the point of imitating others, while the sanguine in her can charm an audience.

She is a very emotional person and subject to the typical black moods of the melancholy. However, the happy side of her sanguine nature usually lifts her spirit so that her depression periods don't last too long. She can also be very creative and learn to express herself in art, music, math, computers, and many other fields.

More verbal than other melancholies, Milly will have to be careful not to hurt others with her criticism or to demotivate others with her pessimism. Especially in a marriage relationship, Milly needs to learn to not audibly correct her husband for meaningless mistakes. After all, it really doesn't matter if the fourth stoplight is eight miles down the road when her husband says it's seven, does it? Milly needs to practice encouraging others and stop correcting unless they ask for her help.

Milly has a wide range of vocational options open to her. For example, the medical profession would be a strong possibility. Her sanguine secondary temperament gives her a good bedside manner, while the perfectionist melancholy in her will provide the best treatment for her patient. She can teach as well as do research, though she may be best suited for the high school or college level.

MelSans often have a good prayer life and enjoy communing with God. Several of the great prophets were probably MelSans. But like all melancholies, Milly will have to work on her great need, and that is practicing thanksgiving as a way of life.

MEET MOLLY MELCHLOR

The many gifts of the melancholy are enriched by the choleric side of this temperament. It is like adding strong will and determination to the most creative of all people. Molly MelChlor has great possibilities in life, but she also may face some serious problems.

Molly can easily become obnoxious, demanding her way which she is usually quick to point out is the best way. Molly can argue endlessly to make a point, whether it is important or not. And she can be very hard or even impossible to please, for she is prone to be rigid and unyielding.

Emotionally, Molly MelChlor can be both angry and fearful, given to fits of deep depression after times of explosion. And because Molly has difficulty forgiving and overlooking insults, affronts, or mistreatment, she can carry a grudge for long periods of time—and she usually has the ulcers or other physical ailments to show for it. She is the happiest when she has a long planning chart laid out in advance for her life. Many MelChlors enjoy pursuing a medical career because it allows them to know where they are going for a long time. Their intelligence enables them to endure the years of learning necessary in most medical fields, while their choleric leadership may thrust them into an administrative or organizational role in the medical field.

In marriage, Molly's weaknesses may make her such a nitpicker that life becomes miserable for her husband who is never able to measure up to her standards. If she isn't careful, Molly can even reduce her sexual expressions to a reward for good behavior. And since her standards of perfection are naturally so high, Molly's husband may live with sexual frustrations.

Molly's weaknesses, like her gifts, are quite similar. To overcome them, she needs to learn to not be so hard on other people and, instead, reach out to them with encouragement. Everyone but the MelChlor knows that encouragement and approval are better motivators than criticism and condemnation. Molly also needs to bring her thoughts into obedience to Christ, learning thanksgiving and concentrating on others more than herself. She needs to gain victory over both anger and fear to avoid ending life as Moses did. Because of Moses' weaknesses, he died before his work was done. But by walking in the Spirit, Molly MelChlor's weaknesses will be transformed.

Meet Mary MelPhleg

One of the quietest of all the temperaments is Mary MelPhleg. The only one more quiet is the superintroverted Phyllis PhlegMel. Mary is not given to explosive anger like other melancholy blends, but she is often driven by excessive fears, worries, anxieties, and feelings of inadequacy. Mary MelPhleg is extremely gifted, but her gifts are usually only manifested in a familiar setting. That is one reason Mary becomes a perpetual student. She is familiar with the academic world and does well there. Rarely will Mary venture out into something new, for she much prefers to remain active in her comfort zone. The thought of change threatens Mary, so she may miss out on many opportunities open to her. As such, it is not uncommon for Mary MelPhleg to remain single all her life. She may have several chances to marry, but because "Mr. Perfect never came by" or the prospect of change doesn't appeal to her, she will remain single.

MelPhlegs may be the most emotional of all people, and since they have such creative minds, it is essential they learn to control their emotions. Otherwise, they will develop the habit of magnifying difficulties and minimizing resources. Once MelPhlegs start thinking negatively and anticipating all kinds of fearful results of their decisions and actions, they will be drawn like quicksand ever downward. Then if an unfortunate or unexpected tragedy does occur, Mary MelPhleg will easily allow it to become a major negative event. For Mary, it is absolutely essential that she live by faith and learn to praise and thank the Lord by faith, even though it is difficult.

Making decisions is difficult for a MelPhleg woman, unless she has a husband who is a strong leader to lean on, and who will encourage her. On her own, Mary MelPhleg will anticipate every negative result of her decision in advance. Instead, she needs to quit counting the cost and anticipate that God will be with her supplying her needs once she gets going. Like all temperaments, Mary needs to decide what the will of the Lord is in a situation and then go do it.

Mary MelPhleg, like several of the Marys in the Bible, has the potential to be a real servant. Mary finds her best sense of self-worth when she is helping people, if she doesn't destroy it all by griping mentally, verbally, or both. Many of the prophets and other servants God used in the Bible were MelPhlegs. But their great contribution came only when they were motivated by the Holy Spirit.

MEET PHYLLIS PHLEGMEL

One of the nicest people you will ever meet is Phyllis PhlegMel. She is a superintrovert with far more natural capability than she realizes. If her negative, fearful thinking pattern doesn't become a habitual way of life, Phyllis can be a blessing in her home, church, and neighborhood. Her calm and easygoing spirit makes her a joy to work with, and she rarely runs into conflict with other people unless they are too insistent that she get involved. Like all phlegmatics, Phyllis PhlegMel is engaged in a lifetime battle to keep from getting too involved in crusades or causes.

For spiritual reasons, Phyllis can overcome her natural fears and, if she begins early in life, she can learn to work with and minister to children. For she is a good teacher once committed. She would never come to class unprepared and would take seriously what others think of her. Although she does not like to take the lead in anything, Phyllis PhlegMel is a good support person.

Phyllis enjoys detail and can learn quickly to produce projects which would drive extroverts up the wall. Phyllis usually has a good mind but will rarely argue or assert herself. She can be so passive that, although starved for love and approval by her husband, she may stick with him, even in the face of verbal or physical abuse. Often she will go along with others' plans because she doesn't want to cause trouble, even though her plan may be far better. Phyllis also works well under pressure; in fact, she probably does not work much unless pressured or committed. It is a wise PhlegMel who realizes that she is externally motivated. By realizing that, she can take on more that she ordinarily would, enabling her to be more productive. Except for her worries, fears, and anxieties, Phyllis rarely has emotional problems. However, like all of us, being in an indecisive mode too long upsets her, for she loves to have decisions, duties, and expectations clearly defined.

Selfishness is one area Phyllis is constantly wrestling with, but not always winning. But once she learns that giving herself away for the Lord's sake is the greatest way to live, she will be motivated to get more involved. This in turn will help Phyllis like herself more. As she matures in life, Phyllis will usually become a happy and fulfilled person, particularly if she has several children into whom she can pour her life. Like all temperaments, she functions best when committed to God and allowing Him to strengthen her and give her courage.

MEET PATTY PHLEGCHLOR

Patty PhlegChlor is an interesting illustration of contrasts blended together, all of which make a very nice person. Patty is the most active of the phlegmatics and is loved by all who know her. She is basically of a quiet spirit with a streak of self-determination, which may at times border on stubbornness. But she is never unreasonable when demanding her own way, because that is not her style. Patty PhlegChlor is content to manipulate and scheme to gain her way.

Patty knows what is right to do and insists on doing it that way. But instead of taking people on in open confrontation, she is more likely to drag her feet until she wears out the patience of an opponent. As a Christian, Patty never blows her top, although she can so aggravate others (in a nice way, of course) that they blow theirs. This action leaves her with some sadistic satisfaction since she comes away looking more Christian and her opponent more carnal.

Of her strengths, few are Patty's equal when it comes to organization. She rarely begins a project until she has all her materials, tools, and plans well in advance. While she is not the most productive person, there is a quality about Patty's unfinished product that you can trust.

Patty PhlegChlor has the best leadership qualities of all the phlegmatics. Her choleric tendencies blended with her phlegmatic organization skills enable her to lead a group or organization in an admirably smooth style. We at Concerned Women for America often find that this blend makes some of our most successful leaders. Such leadership provides an enjoyable work environment, for Patty works well with people. So it is not uncommon for her to have a very productive department of happy employees. And if a homemaker, Patty's family will love the well-organized and efficient home she provides them.

More venturesome than other phlegmatics, Patty PhlegChlor will find it easier than pure phlegmatics to learn to walk by faith and not limit God by unbelief. But in spite of her choleric tendencies, remember: Phlegmatics all have a fear problem. She will not be as dominated by it as others might, however, and particularly if she learns to walk in the Spirit.

Many PhlegChlors are active in their church, but they almost never volunteer or initiate projects. Other people usually have to envision, recruit, and train them. But once they gain confidence in doing a particular job, they may do it faithfully for years to come.

Meet Penny PhlegSan

Penny PhlegSan may just be the easiest person in the world to get along with, but she may live her entire life without much accomplishment if she is not careful. She can be trained to do almost anything, as long as it doesn't involve much assertiveness, for she has the greatest trouble with self-discipline and involvement. You may recognize Penny PhlegSan as the woman who has sat on the church pew for 50 years, rarely missed a service, but who never assumed a leadership role. This is not because Penny is not dedicated to Christ; on the contrary, she may be extremely dedicated, but her problem is fear. Both phlegmatics and sanguines have a problem with fear. So, if she doesn't have something to be afraid of, you can count on Penny to find a reason (or really, an excuse). If anyone needs to trust in the Lord with all her heart, it is Penny. Never too convinced of her own ability, Penny is so afraid of ridicule or public failure that she would rather hide behind her more forceful mate and live her entire life in his shadow.

Penny can be the world's best mother, particularly in the early years of her children's lives. But because she avoids confrontation, when her children become teenagers, Penny may lose control of them. Unless her husband fully backs her, insisting that their children honor and obey their parents as the Scriptures command, the children may become self-willed and rebel against her and God. If she refuses to confront her children as they are developing, Penny could have some disastrous results on her hands. She needs to concentrate on their training rather than on living so they will "like" her. As parents, we all have to exert what has been called "tough love" on our children. And although it is never easy for anyone, it is especially difficult for Penny PhlegSan. But one thing Penny's children can never honestly accuse her of is not loving them, for she always has time for them. And that is truly an admirable trait in a parent.

Many areas of service are open to the PhlegSan who will walk in the Spirit and refuse to limit God by unbelief. When faith replaces her fears, the PhlegSan will begin to realize that God can use her life, for He has created her to be a very capable and productive person. But don't expect her to volunteer or to take giant steps of faith initially. Rather, Penny needs to be lovingly encouraged to trust God and take one step of faith after another. But it will be the first step that is the hardest for Penny.

The church, the home, children, and husbands have seen their lives enriched by the gentle, consistent loving hand of Penny PhlegSan. May their tribe increase!

Meet Cindy ChlorSan

Whenever you mix an extrovert temperament with a superextrovert, you are going to end up with a powerful personality. Cindy ChlorSan is one such powerful personality. She is the strongest natural leader of all the temperament combinations and is usually the one who involuntarily takes over any group or organization in which she is involved. Cindy is a highly opinionated person and has enough extroversion to state what she thinks before others announce their ideas. It also doesn't take her long to realize that she can intimidate others into accepting her ideas simply by stating her case first in positive, unequivocal terms—in such positive terms that anyone offering an objection would almost think their ideas are inferior or unnecessary. Cindy ChlorSan is so powerful that, when she presents her will, it is often hard to tell whether she is speaking on behalf of her will or God's.

Cindy ChlorSan is not only powerful, but is also determined to have her way. In fact, one of her greatest spiritual problems is distinguishing her will for the group (or for her family) from God's. Prayer is not her thing by nature; she is more inclined to act than pray. Most ChlorSans only pray for the big things in life (those things over which they have no control). They tend to think that the smaller, everyday issues of life can be tackled by them, and then they can move ahead. ChlorSans need humbling, which usually takes a series of tribulations and frustrating experiences before they genuinely learn to lean on God.

Cindy ChlorSan does have charm from the sanguine side of her nature, and she generally uses that charm to get married. She will find a quiet, somewhat passive phlegmatic man and charm him to the altar with dogged determination, convinced that after they get married she will make something out of him. But then Cindy will discover that she is in a "push-pull relationship," where she explodes emotionally and he withdraws into his thick shell of self-protection. Because he is no match for her verbally, Cindy's husband will often resort to the weapon of silence. The harder she pushes and tries to lead, the more he digs his feet in and sings to himself, "I shall not be moved." This is not exactly a formula for happiness.

Emotionally, Cindy needs to seek God to overcome her angry, explosive temperament. She needs to apologize to those she offends and to do what the Lord wants for her life more than what she wants. It takes ChlorSans longer than other people to realize that God's way, not theirs, is the path to happiness. But Cindy ChlorSan desperately needs to learn that God does not need her—rather, she needs Him.

ChlorSan women today are most likely to find fulfillment in vocational pursuits outside the home. Invariably, however, this takes a toll on the children. Having mother around constantly in the first years of life is absolutely essential for proper development and a sense of personal security in children. But because business is much more attractive to the ChlorSan wife and mother than homemaking, Cindy ChlorSan will often try to justify her decisions to do what she really wants to do. Too often, she finds a more likable challenge in working outside the home than in being a stay-at-home mom. Sadly, this is often to the detriment of her husband and children.

Cindy ChlorSans are very capable, energetic people who have a strong will, but also have much to offer God. But it is only when they learn to walk in the Spirit and not in the flesh that they can be fully used. For Cindy and her family, it is a happy day when she finally learns that in the end, God's will is always best.

MEET CARRIE CHLORMEL

Carrie ChlorMel is an extremely industrious and

capable person. She is smarter than most, and has a practical bent to her nature that enables her to be successful at just about everything she attempts to do. She is a strong natural leader and usually has a well-defined plan of attack. But unless she is leading an army into battle, Carrie's leadership often costs her more than it is worth because of her tendency to run people over or even destroy them in the process of winning. Very simply, by nature Carrie ChlorMel is a very insensitive person.

Many ChlorMels have become leaders in Concerned Women for America. These women are deeply concerned Christians who clearly see the terrible threat liberal humanism is having on our culture. They are motivated, energetic women who are eager to take on the task of leadership. But the biggest problem we have with some of them is in helping them learn to be gracious, kind, and Christlike in the way they deal with less-aggressive members. We also strive to help them learn that the best way to oppose the enemies of the home is through a gracious attitude, for confrontation often leads to greater confrontation. Many senators and congressmen tell me that our CWA ladies across the country have clout. While we appreciate that sentiment, we want our leaders to be known as gracious ladies who have clout. Look at the angry, hostile feminists, and you can understand why they drive more women to become members of CWA. When these people join, they shouldn't be confronted by angry, hostile Christian women who speak with the same bitterness as the feminists. Instead, we want these new members to meet Spirit-filled women who are gracious and deeply committed to preserving the Christian principles that made America the greatest nation in history.

Unfortunately, ChlorMels often get so engrossed in their work or projects that they neglect their friends, husband, and family, and even lash out at them if they complain. Carrie ChlorMel will make a happier life for herself and her friends and family when she learns the biblical principle that it is " 'not by might nor by power [nor by Carrie ChlorMel's effort and skill], but by My Spirit,' says the LORD." Like all temperaments, Carrie ChlorMel must learn to become dependent on the Holy Spirit. The apostle Paul is probably the greatest illustration of a Spirit-filled workaholic in the Bible. Unfortunately, you won't find many such ChlorMel Christian servants like him, and that is probably because ChlorMels have such a difficult time submitting their will, flesh, and emotions to God. Even in Paul's case, it took the Damascus experience to bring his strong will into God's control.

Carrie ChlorMel is often feared, sometimes respected, but not always well liked. She often has an abrasive personality and doesn't care that others know it. But many times you will find Carrie whining "No one likes me" or asking why she doesn't have more friends. What Carrie does not realize is that she is often so critical and condemning of other people for their actions or plans that no one likes being around her.

ChlorMels are women who can turn off men, but particularly they can turn off women. Put together a

woman's more talkative nature with a choleric's opinionated personality and a melancholy's detailed, perfectionist nature, and you have a woman who can talk
and argue people and projects to death. But while they
often win the argument, they lose the relationship.
Consequently, only when a ChlorMel woman realizes
that she must submit to her husband's authority and
give him respect (Ephesians 5:33) will she have a Christian home and a happy relationship. Submission is
hard for any ChlorMel, but this again points out how
dependent and necessary the ministry of the Holy
Spirit is in Carrie's life.

MEET CAROLYN CHLORPHLEG

One of the most organized women you will ever
meet is Carolyn ChlorPhleg. Carolyn has a desire for
the surface organization of the choleric ("a place for
everything and everything in its place") and for the
detailed organization of the phlegmatic. No one runs a
neater household than Carolyn, all the while working
on a dozen other projects. If you need a job done that
requires motivating and directing other people, few
can do it better. She has just enough of the gracious
phlegmatic temperament to tone down the demanding choleric side of her nature so she can be both a doer
and a people person. ChlorPhleg women are often
able to climb the ladder in business because they are
natural-born leaders and are quite efficient.

Unfortunately, many churches don't utilize the talents of many Carolyn ChlorPhlegs. This may be because
Carolyn is not always interested in God's will for her
life or because Christians tire of her caustic barbs. Still

other people find it hard to think that anyone as sarcastic as Carolyn ChlorPhleg would be spiritual enough to hold a leadership role. Sometimes if Carolyn does receive a leadership role, she alienates so many people that it is a short-term assignment. Consequently, Carolyn will usually look outside of the church for work activity. Civic clubs are, for example, often more accepting of her blunt and sometimes carnal nature.

Carolyn is given to activism, as all cholerics are, but her activity has purpose and meaning and she knows intuitively what needs to be done and the fastest and shortest way to do it. So once Carolyn becomes committed to Christ and is introduced to the eternal work of God, it is hard for her to settle for anything short of Christian service. And with her seemingly boundless energy, if she can't find a place of service, she will probably start one.

Like most choleric women, Carolyn ChlorPhleg will have a hard time learning to "submit to her husband as unto the Lord." To her credit, once she gets that message and understands that she cannot be a spiritual wife unless she does submit to her husband, she will have a lasting and happy marriage. Only then will she reap the blessings of a life filled with godly submission.

MEET SHIRLEY SANCHLOR

The strongest extrovert of all the blends of temperaments is Shirley SanChlor, for she is made up of the two most powerful extrovertish temperaments. Since the sanguine temperament predominates, Shirley is a happy individual who has charisma to burn. She is a people-oriented person who, when filled with the Holy Spirit, is loved by everyone and has a real ministry of leading others to Christ. I have seen many SanChlor women leading Christian women's organizations or teaching Bible study groups. The choleric side of her nature provides the necessary self-discipline and resolution that will enable her to give a favorable first impression. And her organized and consistent discipline to finish a project will make a lasting good impression. Shirley has the capacity to lift everyone's spirit around her and is genuinely a fun, loving person. As a public speaker, Shirley is much in demand, as much for her sense of humor and ready wit as for her practical motivational skills.

Shirley's weaknesses, like those of all extroverts, are as apparent as her strengths. Like most sanguines, she suffers from the tendency to gain weight. She tends to blame her weight problem on "having four children" or "gland trouble." But if you watch her, you will often find that Shirley eats too fast, too much, and loves rich foods that are high in fat grams and calories. Another weakness is that she talks too much, as most extroverts do. In so doing, Shirley ends up exposing the depth of her thinking. Unfortunately, as is true of many sanguines, Shirley's thinking isn't very deep. Consequently, her repeated jokes and stories wear thin. No one has more mouth trouble than Shirley SanChlor.

Emotionally, Shirley will have a problem with anger most of her life, unless she goes to the Holy Spirit for the cure that He alone can provide. Shirley will also cry without provocation and then repent easily, not only because she is so spontaneous, but also because she has had so much practice. For an illustration of a Bible character who was a SanChlor, study the life of the apostle Peter. Before he was filled with the Holy Spirit, Peter had more intent to do right than he had resolve to do it. But after yielding his life to the Lord, he became a great servant of God.

If she gets control of her mouth and allows the Holy Spirit to develop her self-discipline, Shirley San-Chlor can become a lovable person who will enjoy the love of friends and family. But like all other blends of temperament, Shirley needs to walk daily in the control of the Spirit of God.

MEET SANDY SANMEL

While no temperament is a stronger extrovert than Shirley SanChlor, no temperament combination is more emotional than Sandy SanMel. As we have seen, sanguines are emotionally expressive and melancholies are deeply sensitive. So when blended together, the result is a highly emotional person. Typically Sandy SanMel will leave her friends emotionally wrung out. One minute she will be crying compassionately with someone, and seconds later she will be laughing with or exploding in anger at another person. This emotional variation often gains her the reputation of being insincere, when in reality she is just being sincerely sanguine. Surprisingly, Sandy rarely has a nervous breakdown—she just gives them to others. She can't carry a grudge, and her down moods only last until someone comes by to cheer her up or challenge her with something she wants to do. Sandy also enjoys music; in fact, she can hardly live without it. If she is discerning about the kind of music she listens to, she will rarely experience depression for very long. For example, if she plays praise and worship music, she will have an upbeat spirit. If, however, Sandy indulges a down mood and plays mournful-sounding music, then her sensitive spirit will plunge into deep despair for a much longer time than is natural for sanguines.

No one feels the grief and emotional hurts of others like Sandy SanMel. She usually has a good ministry to those with hurts and feels comfortable in their presence. Vocationally, almost any field is open to Sandy, from music or acting to sales or public speaking. Sandy must guard her tongue, however, because sanguines will say almost anything that enters their mind, and melancholies are critical thinkers who will find fault with almost everyone. Consequently, she can hurt others unnecessarily by saying everything that comes to mind. So she must dedicate herself to only saying those things that edify and encourage. Sandy's ego tendencies also make indulging in silence for any length of time difficult, so she needs to be careful about saying anything that is unnecessary and hurtful.

One area that SanMels have to work on is their thought life. Both sanguines and melancholies are dreamers. So consequently, if the melancholy side suggests a negative thought or policy, it can negate the sanguine optimism. And in addition, both temperaments are insecure and fearful. So Sandy will really need to work on becoming a woman of the Word and learn to walk by faith under the control of the Spirit in order to accomplish her great potential. God has used many SanMels. One outstanding example that comes to mind is David, the talented, personable sweet psalmist of Israel, the man "after God's own heart." But Sandy needs to be aware that her powerful emotional nature makes her vulnerable to sensual temptation, just as King David was. That road will only lead to pain and is spiritually unnecessary, even in these sensually surcharged days. If Sandy will seek righteousness with all her heart and keep her mind centered only on that which is pleasing to the Lord, she will overcome the temptations around her.

MEET SUSIE SANPHLEG

The easiest person in the world to like is Susie San-Phleg. Her overpowering, superextrovert sanguine tendencies are offset by her gracious, easygoing, never-get-upset phlegmatic traits. Susie SanPhleg is usually a very happy person whose carefree spirit and good humor make her a lighthearted entertainer who is sought after by others. Helping other people is her chief business in life, and when she consecrates her life to Christ, she gets her greatest joy out of serving Him. She often loves music and may be a moving and effective singer. If I were a church choir director, I would put all SanPhlegs in the front row because their smiling countenances and joy-filled appearance usually blesses the congregation even before the choir begins to sing.

Family life is very important to Susie SanPhleg. If she is given loving approval by her husband, she will love him devotedly and will adore her children. And because Susie is personally undisciplined, it is not unusual for her to overindulge her children. Otherwise she makes a very loving mother, and with very little encouragement from her mate, she can be a marvelous entertainer. Two women in our church who had the best results with hospitality evangelism were a SanPhleg and a SanChlor, both of whom had cooperative husbands.

Knowing your primary temperament and secondary (if possible) is helpful, but only if you go to the Holy Spirit to help you confront your weaknesses.

No one is equipped by God to be a greater hostess and naturally sociable than Susie SanPhleg. She would rather talk and fellowship than anything else. To Susie's credit, when she has been properly trained, God can use her to be a real soul-winner. She does have a problem with fear, though. But like many people in the Bible, when she is dependent on the Word of God and the filling of the Holy Spirit, Susie will be a consistent and disciplined Christian who will accomplish all that God has for her to do.

ADDITIONAL VARIABLES TO CONSIDER

With 12 temperament blends to choose from, it should be easier for you to identify with one of them than with only the four basic temperaments. Don't be discouraged, however, if you find that you don't quite fit into any one of the 12, either. No two human beings are exactly alike. Many other variables could alter the picture sufficiently so that you will not fit any model precisely. Consider the following:

1. *Your percentages may be different from the 60/40 I arbitrarily chose as a basis for this section.* I think you will agree that it would be nearly impossible to detail all the conceivable mixtures of temperament. I leave that to the reader. For example, a MelChlor of 60/40 will be significantly different from an 80/20 MelChlor. Or consider the disparity between a 55/45 SanPhleg and an 85/15 SanPhleg. Only detailed scientific testing can establish an accurate diagnosis.

2. *Different backgrounds and childhood training alter the expressions of identical temperament blends.* For example, a SanPhleg raised by loving but firm parents will be much more disciplined than one raised by permissive parents. In the same manner, a MelPhleg brought up by cruel, hateful parents will be drastically different from one raised by tender, understanding parents. Both will share the same strengths and talents, but one may be overcome with hostility, depression, and self-persecution, so that she never uses her strengths. Because each person's upbringing wields a powerful influence, it is all but impossible to assess a wide variety of backgrounds in such a temperament analysis as this.

3. *You may not be objective when looking at yourself.* Therefore, you may wish to discuss your temperament with loved ones and friends. All of us tend to view ourselves through rose-colored glasses. To paraphrase

the yearning of the poet Robert Burns: "Oh, to see ourselves as others see us."

4. *Education and IQ will often influence the appraisal of a person's temperament.* For example, a MelSan with a very high IQ will appear somewhat different from one who is average or lower in intelligence. Even so, if you carefully study the strengths and weaknesses of people of a particular temperament blend, you will find them to be basically similar in their strengths and weaknesses in spite of different IQ, educational, or experience levels.

5. *Health and metabolism are important.* A ChlorPhleg in top physical condition will be more aggressive than one with a faulty thyroid gland or other physical ailment. A nervous PhlegMel will also be more active than one who is suffering from low blood pressure.

6. *A few people will find that none of the 12 blends fits them.* In such cases, they will predominate in one temperament and have the tendencies of two others. However, of all the testing my husband has done, less than ten percent of people fit into this category.

7. *Motivation is the name of the game!* "Out of [the heart] spring the issues of life" (Proverbs 4:23). If a person is properly motivated, it will have a marked impact on her behavior regardless of her temperament blend. Actually, that is why I have written this book— so people who are improperly motivated at present will experience the power of God to completely transform their behavior.

8. *The Spirit-controlled life is a behavior modifier.* Mature Christians whose temperaments have been

modified by the Holy Spirit often find it difficult to analyze their temperamental makeup because they make the mistake of examining the temperament theory in light of their present behavior. Temperament is based on the natural man; there is nothing spiritual about it. That is why we find it so much easier to diagnose and classify an unsaved person or a carnal Christian than a dedicated, mature Christian. Because a mature Christian will already have had many of her natural weaknesses overcome, it is difficult to assess her temperament. She should either concentrate only on her strengths or consider her behavior before she became a Spirit-controlled believer.

Knowing your primary temperament and secondary (if possible) is helpful, but only if you go to the Holy Spirit to help you confront your weaknesses. And that is what the rest of this book will help you do. You then can be the kind of godly woman who will glorify the Lord and receive much happiness.

10

Singleness Is Not a Curse

*W*e women are fortunate that God is not a respec-
ter of age, sex, or position. He is able to be all-
sufficient for single as well as married women,
for young as well as older. We all have spent at least
part of our lives as singles, although some more than
others. And some people may have a life of singleness,
while others may be married for a season and then
become single again. Being single again can be the
result of a divorce or the death of a spouse. But we have
all been given the same instruction, regardless of our
marital status: "If we live in the Spirit, let us also walk
in the Spirit" (Galatians 5:25).

The time-honored idea that one must be an older
married woman in order to be a Spirit-filled Christian
is not necessarily true. The Holy Spirit does not select
only mature Christians to fulfill the promises of God.
God's promises are available to anyone who is willing
to completely yield her life to the Lord.

Tender Teenager

Years ago when our children were very young, we had a teenage girl come to babysit for our family one evening. When we returned home that night, there was time for a short visit with her. We asked about school, her family, etc., and then talked to her about her relationship with Christ. She quickly responded, "I'm a Christian, but I don't want to get too spiritual and that stuff until I get older. I want to enjoy myself while I'm young." We watched her as she struggled through her teens and prayed that God would build a hedge of protection around her. On several occasions she came very close to scarring her young adult life. Many years later this same girl told us how sorry she was that she had wasted so many years of her life and how she had come close to ruining it.

Teenage girls can be Spirit-filled and still have a wonderful social life! I have seen many examples of this in the young people who have gone through our own church. It is a beautiful witness to see a lovely, vivacious teenage girl who is completely committed to Jesus Christ. One girl in particular comes to my mind. She was neither beautiful nor ugly; in fact, she was rather plain and average. This gal was a steady witness for Christ and was liked by all her peers. The males especially liked her because of her gentle, friendly nature. She had problems that would cause some teenagers to buckle under, but not her. Instead, she had committed every area of her life, problems and all, to Jesus Christ. Was she a social outcast? Not on your life! She was totally committed to Christ and truly a Spirit-controlled teenage gal. Her ability to show her genuine interest in other people rather than focusing on her own problems was a testimony of Christ living in her life.

❧ ─────────────────────

Dating is a critical time to check your temperament weaknesses lest you allow your emotions to lead your heart. You need to have clearly established convictions before you dare to date.

───────────────────── ❧

I had seen two problem areas of her life change completely during her teen years. One was her relationship with her parents. A rebellious girl is not a Spirit-filled Christian. The Bible clearly states, "Children, obey your parents" and "Honor thy father and mother." When she desired to please God in all things, it was necessary for her to commit her rebellious spirit to God and to obey His plan for respecting her parents. She now has a very happy mom and dad, and together they have developed a beautiful relationship.

The other area that drastically changed was her self-acceptance. When she realized that God accepted her as she was, problems and all, she began to change her ideas. She had been measuring herself by the world's yardstick. Her vision had been blurred by the bitterness and resentment she felt toward her Creator. But when other things in her life were confessed and corrected, she began to accept the fact that she was a custom-made individual, prepared for a specific purpose by the hand of God.

DARE TO DATE

Your dating years are a time in your feminine life that should be entered into very cautiously and with wise guidance. This is a critical time to check your temperament weaknesses lest you allow your emotions to lead your heart. You need to have clearly established convictions before you dare to date. The ground rules should be made in your own mind before you ever leave home. It is too late to try to decide what rules to play by when you find yourself in the middle of a clinch in a parked car. God has definite ideas on dating. Remember that you are a child for whom God gave His only Son. Does He care whom you date, where you go, and how you conduct yourself? He surely does! If your desire is to have a Spirit-controlled dating life, then you must consider what God desires for you. Second Corinthians 6:14 speaks very clearly about the kind of man God wants you to marry: "Do not be unequally yoked together with unbelievers. For what fellowship has righteousness with lawlessness? And what communication has light with darkness?"

Of course, we are talking about dating and not marriage, but the two are definitely related. One sure way to prevent marrying a non-Christian is to never date a non-Christian.

When God said, "Children, obey your parents," He certainly had in mind teenage girls and young women. If your mom and dad have rules and standards for your dating, then thank God for parents who love you and want to guard against the temptations that surround you during this period in your life. When a fellow helps you obey your dating rules, it shows real strength of character on his part. Beware of the young man who encourages you to cheat on the dating rules that your parents have established for you. If your parents have not established guidelines to protect you, then lay out the godly standards you want for your life—and keep them. If you have any question about how far you should go in a sexual relationship before marriage, I want to encourage you to seek out your minister or a godly counselor. Concerned Women for America has produced a wonderful video for teens on abstinence entitled "Wait for Me." This video gives honest answers on why you should wait for marriage before you have sex. It helps a young lady to know how to say "no."

One of our daughters came to a crossroad in her dating life when she had to make a decision between obeying her parents and pleasing her date. This boy seemed to bristle under the dating rules we set for our daughter. Time and time again he would call on the phone and try to rearrange things and get us to bend our rules this way or that. It put our daughter under a great deal of pressure, and tension seemed to mount between us every time he would call. Finally, our daughter decided she had had enough and told him that he had to make a choice—either to date her with her parents' rules just as they were or not to date her at all. The young man decided after several days not to date her anymore. He boldly stated that she was used to more discipline than he and that he just didn't want to be put under that pressure.

This was not a happy time for our daughter, but spiritually she grew two feet that day. To us it proved that the young man was not really meant for our daughter, anyway. We wanted her to marry a man with the strength of character and discipline necessary to do the thing that was right even when it wasn't his choice. We have learned that young people who rebel against their parents' rules are prone to rebel against God and eventually each other.

BEFORE YOU SAY "I DO"

"Therefore do not be unwise, but understand what the will of the Lord is" (Ephesians 5:17).

When you fall in love, it becomes difficult to always think straight and to be objective regarding the Lord's will for your life. The time to start seeking God's leading is before love begins; once you're in love, your heart can play tricks on you. Since you will probably fall in love only with someone you have dated, ask God at the very start whom you should date. Following this plan will keep you on the right path and will help you to be objective as you choose your partner for life.

What kind of a man should you consider marrying? Just looking for a tall, dark, and handsome man is not good enough. There will come a day when those features may change, and that handsome man may look more like a maturing beach ball. All young men with handsome features will not necessarily be good marriage partners. Your "dream man" will be one you must sit across the table from day after day. He will be there to see you at your best moments and at your worst. There will be days when he will not be the man of your dreams—unless they are nightmares. But you will marry him "for better or for worse, for richer or for poorer, in sickness and in health, till death do us part." On those days his height, shade of complexion, and good looks will have nothing to do with whether he is a good husband day after day and year after year.

What is this man really like? Look beyond his outward appearance and consider the real inner person:

> Is he a man of good character and integrity?
>
> What is his relationship to Jesus Christ?
>
> Is he active in a good Bible-believing church?
>
> What is his attitude about regular Bible study?
>
> Does he respect the standards and rules of your parents?
>
> Is he kind and thoughtful to others?
>
> How does he treat his mother?
>
> Does he talk only about himself?
>
> How much interest does he show in your needs and concerns?
>
> Is he able to control his physical attraction toward you?
>
> Does he consider your reputation and value your moral convictions and standards?
>
> Does he treat you like a lady?

Is he ready to love you as much as he
loves himself?

Scripture clearly defines in Ephesians 5:25-33 what
a great responsibility a husband is to have for his wife:

> Husbands, love your wives, just as Christ
> also loved the church and gave Himself for
> it, that He might sanctify and cleanse it
> with the washing of water by the word. . . .
> So husbands ought to love their own wives
> as their own bodies; he who loves his wife
> loves himself. . . . "For this reason a man
> shall leave his father and mother and be
> joined to his wife, and the two shall become
> one flesh." . . . Nevertheless let each one of
> you in particular so love his own wife as
> himself, and let the wife see that she respects
> her husband.

Now is the time to look him over carefully. Ask any
and all of the questions you might have. It is far better
to ask now than to wish you had in years to come.

Of all the temperaments, Martha Melancholy is
more likely to ask questions and ask questions and ask
questions. She is looking for the perfect man! She may
fall in love with someone she thinks is the "ideal
man," but then finds out that he is human and has a
few weaknesses. She will then be inclined to break the
engagement and call off the wedding. But this is far
better than leaving him after the wedding is over.
However, she needs to understand the Holy Spirit is

able to help them both overcome their weaknesses. After all, she has weaknesses, too! How beautiful it is when a young couple can prayerfully enter a wedding relationship together, asking for the filling of the Spirit to blend their strengths and weaknesses and unite them as one.

Martha may be mistaken as an unfriendly snob when really she is not. Because she is withdrawn and tends to be a loner, she gives the impression of being unfriendly. Boys feel uncomfortable around her and may not be too eager to ask her for a date. Her personality and social life would be greatly improved if she could trust God to help her develop a friendly, more outgoing spirit.

Polly Phlegmatic is likely to have several boyfriends because she is so easygoing and pleasant to be with. However, Polly is very timid and lacks confidence. Of all the temperaments, she will probably be the most surprised when her future husband proposes, wondering why he ever wanted her.

In a survey that my husband and I conducted in preparation for our book *The Act of Marriage*, we discovered that the phlegmatic woman engaged in premarital sex far more than the phlegmatic man. Because she is usually involved with a man of stronger temperament and is eager to please, Polly is more likely to give in even against her convictions. It is at this point that she desperately needs the discerning wisdom of the Holy Spirit to sort out what is right and wrong. But there is no need for her to be swept along with the emotions of her lover. God can stabilize and help her to evaluate the total picture before she makes a final commitment to her prospective husband.

Clara Choleric may likely be the girl who wants to get married quickly and get on with life. She is inclined to rush into marriage without ever analyzing the pros and cons or evaluating her relationship and future with this man. She is probably confident that she will be able to tackle whatever problems she may face. Her greatest need at this time is to slow down and wait for the leading of the Holy Spirit. However, Clara is so dynamic she will have a tendency to drive young men away, since her dominant spirit could be a threat to young men. God has a plan for her, and Clara must learn to move according to His time schedule.

Sarah Sanguine is such a lover by nature that she will probably fall in and out of love several times before she ever settles down. She is so friendly and outgoing that many boys mistake her for a flirt and are swept off their feet. A girl has to learn the difference between being a flirt and genuine friendliness. Somewhere Sarah has to find a happy medium where she can be truly free, instead of inhibited, self-conscious, or overly aggressive. God's love in her life will be reflected in her genuine, warm friendliness and her gracious spirit and will give her the proper balance in her friendships. But because Sarah is often naive and childlike, she needs a special hedge of protection built around her by the Holy Spirit. She can easily be talked into anything and could make a wrong decision that would affect her entire life. Her sympathetic and compassionate heart could lead her to marry because of sympathy and not love. Sarah needs to be Spirit-filled, as all temperaments do, but she especially needs divine help in developing strong convictions and the strength of character to live by them.

THOUGHTLESS TEMPTATION

I may be walking on thin ice with the next subject, but nevertheless, I feel compelled to proceed. It is so easy for a young woman to turn a guy on and not be fully aware of what she is doing. Sadly, many Christian girls and women are rather thoughtless about this. I have seen lovely girls clothe and conduct themselves in such a manner that they turn fellows on and cause them to have problems with lust and evil thoughts. Often the response is that this is the young man's problem and not the woman's. But is it really? True, a Christian man has to overcome the temptation to lust after a woman, but I believe that God holds the woman accountable for the manner in which she dresses and conducts herself.

One charming young lady was walking out of church with her hand on her date's arm and was very carelessly allowing her breast to rub against the boy. Is it possible that she was not even aware of what she was doing to him? Well perhaps, but I believe if she is alive she is fully aware. On another occasion I saw a darling girl cuddled next to her date in church. But during the sermon she reached over and placed her hand on his upper leg and rubbed it tenderly. It looked very innocent, but I could almost hear the fireworks going off in the sex organs of the young man.

One thing that every girl should keep in mind is that her body is the temple of the Holy Spirit. Second Corinthians 6:16 says, "And what agreement has the temple of God with idols? For you are the temple of the living God. As God has said: 'I will dwell in them and walk among them. I will be their God, and they shall be My people.'"

You are not the owner of your own body. If you are a Christian, you have been bought with a price; therefore, you should glorify God with your body.

This leads to another subject: How do you dress? There are three categories in dress: 1) the suggestive, sexy fashions that seduce; 2) the liberated style which neither seduces nor attracts, allowing the woman to express her rebellion; or 3) the modest, feminine approach that sends the message that you are proud to be a woman, but that you also want to be modest and attractive. The sexy approach is represented by very short and tight miniskirts, skin-tight pants or sweaters, the no-bra look, and plunging necklines. All this leaves little to the male imagination and results in appearing seductive rather than attractive. To determine if your skirt is too short, sit in a chair in front of a mirror wearing the skirt in question and cross your legs (which is often the way women sit). You decide if this is the impression and image you wish to leave with your friends or strangers. Ask yourself, What is a man to do, what is he to think, or where will he look if I present myself in this manner?

The liberated style can be anything from faded, ragged jeans, to "plain-Jane" or masculine-style clothing. Such styles may gain frequent stares from passersby, but seldom looks of approval. The feminine approach is represented by modest clothing, which is not sexually suggestive, but is stylish, attractive, and presents a feminine mystique. We are to be modest, attractive, appealing, and—most of all—remain feminine as God made us.

Why do you dress the way you do? Seriously consider this and answer honestly. Is it because you feel you are only a sex object and that is all you have that can attract the man you want? If that is your reason, then you do have a problem and lack a high opinion of who you really are! Your appearance will certainly give that away. Or is it because you are glad to be feminine, proud to be a woman, and you want to represent someone with character and discipline in your life? Why am I addressing this subject? Because this book is about Spirit-controlled womanhood and I believe this is a basic hindrance that keeps women from giving the appearance of godliness.

In some cases I believe women are unaware of just what effect clothes have on a man. I met one such woman recently. She was a fine Christian woman, very active in her church program, and probably one of their most faithful weeknight evangelistic callers. However, her choice of clothes began to present a problem to some of the men. She wore extremely short dresses which showed off a major portion of her very shapely legs and, when seated, exposed even more of her upper thigh. Finally, the pastor's wife decided to speak to her privately about the stir she was causing. She prayed that this woman would not be offended, but that she would accept her words in the right spirit. As it turned out, this dear lady had no idea that she was causing a problem or that her clothes were offensive. Her genuine desire was to please the Lord and to be a testimony of Christ living in her. So after thanking the pastor's wife for approaching her in such a gracious manner, she determined to dress in a more modest, Christlike style. That was the response of a Spirit-filled woman!

COMPANIONSHIP OR CONFUSION

Most single working women or college women find it necessary to share an apartment with another girl in order to keep living expenses to a minimum and to provide the fellowship that most of us need. This is the true test of your Spirit-filled life and a good preparation for marriage. It is likely that two opposite temperaments will become roommates—and this could be the beginning of their problems. The sanguine girl is more apt to leave her clothes hooked on doorknobs or over the back of chairs, while the choleric is likely to develop a bossy attitude and try to run the household. Both of these could be a source of many heartaches. There will be some girls who have very definite ideas on how the cooking should be done, where the furniture should be arranged, how clean the apartment should be kept, how to spend the grocery budget, and a host of other differences. This could be a great learning and adjusting period to experience living with other temperaments. But be aware of potential problems at the beginning by knowing your roommate— her temperament, her background, and her spiritual status. Sometimes bad precedents are set at the start of a living situation which women are afraid to break later for fear of hurt feelings.

Many people who have attended the Family Life Seminars my husband and I conducted over the years are singles who have been helped tremendously by the temperament study in learning to live with other people. This study is also good preparation for marriage. It is a matter of learning to give and take, of not always getting your own way, and of being able to accept the weaknesses and strengths of another person. Ask the Lord to give you wisdom and gentleness and, above all, to help you face each moment under the control of the Spirit.

> *It is likely that two opposite temperaments will become roommates—and this could be the beginning of their problems.*

Beware of an improper physical attachment between you and your roommate. Sadly, this does happen in today's world—especially if someone is lonely, overly affectionate, and lacks a sense of security. But this will not happen if you and your roommate are walking in the Spirit and are actively involved in a Bible-believing church. The secret is to be sure your relationship with the Lord is right—be sure He is in first place.

SEX AND STILL A SINGLE WOMAN

Single women at various ages have the same basic sex drives that God put in all human beings. Some fortunate women do not struggle with this as much as others do. But regardless, it is a real struggle in life.

So much in our culture today points toward being involved in a sexual relationship. We are surrounded with the suggestion that this is the norm and everybody is doing it. Unfortunately, more and more opposite-sex singles are choosing to live together. In today's secular community, sex for singles is more or less taken for granted, but God's standards do not change.

Sexual relations with men outside of marriage can be very tempting and readily available for a single woman (young, middle-aged, and senior women included). A recent article in a secular magazine gave some rather alarming statistics about sex at the office. A survey of 2500 secretaries revealed that 40 percent of them were having lunch-hour sex affairs. What motivates secretaries to have sex with their boss if they know there is no chance of marriage? Probably many do so because they are desperately lonely and will pay any price for a period of tenderness even though they know it is only temporary. Or perhaps it is the idea that sex is necessary to keep their job. If that is true, then get out of that job as quickly as possible! God only blesses those who obey His commandments.

An article written by Dr. Robert J. Collins of the Loretto Geriatrics Center of Syracuse, New York, states that one of the basic flaws in the "new morality" is the assumption that male and female sexuality are the same. With the male, sex can be an activity that is completely separated from his whole being, while for the female and her complex emotional system, it is her whole existence. Dr. Collins mentions that women claim that the tender, warm promises and touches are delightful, but the sex act itself usually leads to an "Is that all there is to it?" reaction.

God has given very definite instructions about all of this:

> Do you not know that the unrighteous will not inherit the kingdom of God? Do not be deceived. Neither fornicators, nor idolaters, nor adulterers, nor homosexuals, nor sodomites, nor thieves, nor covetous, nor drunkards, nor revilers, nor extortioners will inherit the kingdom of God. And such were some of you. But you were washed, but you were sanctified, but you were justified in the name of the Lord Jesus and by the Spirit of our God (1 Corinthians 6:9-11).
>
> Now the body is not for sexual immorality but for the Lord, and the Lord for the body (1 Corinthians 6:13).
>
> Flee sexual immorality. Every sin that a man does is outside the body, but he who commits sexual immorality sins against his own body (1 Corinthians 6:18).

Paul says that some of you were adulterers or fornicators, but when you became a Christian you were forgiven, sanctified, and justified in the name of the Lord Jesus and by the Spirit of God. This leaves no exceptions for sex outside of marriage to the woman who desires to be a Spirit-filled person.

Some will think that this is a rather prudish standard because, after all, sex is enjoyable and satisfies a necessary, God-given drive. But one aspect that the world rarely talks about when it advocates free love and promiscuity is the heavy burden of guilt. The Bible teaches that man has a conscience that either accuses him or excuses him, based on his behavior (Romans 2:15). In a practical sense, that accusation renders the ecstasy of the sexual liaison inadequate when compared to the weight of guilt it creates. Whereas the sexual experience only occupies a few moments of time, the burden of guilt must be borne over a lengthy period. Besides the guilt factor is the risk of infection by any one of more than 50 different sexually transmitted diseases, some of which have no cure. The greatest threat, of course, is being infected with the death sentence of the HIV virus. But beyond the diseases lies the fact that it is impossible for any Christian to grow spiritually while violating God's standards of sexual behavior. I have counseled many single women who were experiencing depression and spiritual retardation only to find that the real culprit was the misuse of their sex drive.

God loves you and is interested in your sexual relations. After all, He created sex for you to enjoy at the right time. So it is important not to rush ahead of His proper timing for you. One beautiful Christian woman prayed this prayer, "Lord, help me to preserve my body for the one You are preparing for me, and help him to preserve his body just for me!"

SINGLE AND GROWING OLDER

Somewhere along the road a single woman has to face the fact that it is possible God never meant for her to marry and that she may have been selected to live without marrying for the rest of her life. Since it has been estimated that there are 109 women to every 100 men, it stands to reason that some women will not be able to marry. You may ask whether God can give a woman a full, rich life without marriage. Is He limited just because a woman does not have a husband? Of course not! Our relationship to Christ is on an individual basis. A husband cannot grow spiritually for his wife. In fact, I can think of several instances when a woman might have been more spiritually advanced had it not been for her husband's interference. Nevertheless, you alone determine your relationship to Christ. Let Christ finish what He has begun in you: "Being confident of this very thing, that He who has begun a good work in you will complete it until the day of Jesus Christ" (Philippians 1:6). The love relationship between you and God is forever, not until you marry or until you die.

And if He does call you to a single life, rest assured that He has called you to a special and beautiful relationship with Himself. You will be able to concentrate on serving the Lord and pleasing only Him: "There is a difference between a wife and a virgin. The unmarried woman cares about the things of the Lord, that she may be holy both in body and in spirit. But she who is married cares about the things of the world—how she may please her husband" (1 Corinthians 7:34).

Your local church offers many areas of Christian service to help you enrich your life. Opportunities include teaching a Bible class for other singles, extending Christian hospitality to others in your church, or

getting actively involved in your church's calling ministry. A ministry with younger girls—whether it be
opening your home for teens to have a Bible study,
teaching Sunday school, or helping in the local pregnancy support center, etc.—all of these can be a very
enriching experience. Our one objective in life, our
ultimate desire, should be to bring pleasure to the
heart of God.

> You are worthy, O Lord, to receive glory
> and honor and power; for You created all
> things, and by Your will they exist and were
> created (Revelation 4:11).

> [Jesus said,] For whoever desires to save his
> life will lose it, but whoever loses his life for
> My sake and the gospel's will save it (Mark
> 8:35).

Singlehood at any age is what you make it to be. It
can be a full, rich, and rewarding life or an existence of
self-pity. One 29-year-old woman was so eager to be
married that she scared the guys away. She was obsessed with the idea of getting married so that she
would not be left to spend her life alone. Meanwhile,
her friend, three years her junior and already married,
was having severe marital problems. One night at the
peak of her marital turmoil, this friend left her war-
zone home and went to the single girl's apartment to
spill out her troubles. The older single woman listened
to the married woman for two hours and finally realized that she was not so bad off after all. Her apartment
was not a war zone, but a haven of rest. The walls then

became a place of tranquility instead of a den of loneliness. She learned to be grateful to God for her peace of mind and content where she was.

"For I have learned in whatever state I am, to be content" (Philippians 4:11).

11

Married for Keeps

F

*W*omen have played an important role throughout the history of the world—in spite of what some people would have us believe today. As someone once said, "The hand that rocks the cradle rules the world." Another famous statement to remember is, "Behind every successful man is a great woman."

A woman is a necessary part of a man—a part which makes him fulfilled and complete. God created woman very specially from one of Adam's ribs: "And the LORD God caused a deep sleep to fall on Adam, and he slept; and He took one of his ribs, and closed up the flesh in its place. Then the rib which the LORD God had taken from man He made into a woman, and He brought her to the man" (Genesis 2:21,22).

Woman is a part of man, not a lesser or greater part, but an equal. She is God's provision to give man total fulfillment; likewise, God designed man to be the provider, protector, and lover to the woman. God designed marriage to be dynamic and fulfilling, a relationship where both husband and wife are to be excited about each other. I can honestly say that after 40-plus years of marriage my husband, Tim, is my very best friend—and he still makes me excited. My heart beats faster every time he walks into a room.

ONENESS IN CHRIST

The most important goal for every bride and groom is to learn to follow God's principles for marriage. God's designs are true and they work. We cannot function at our best as individuals if He is not a major part of our lives. Man and woman are basically self-centered individuals, and marriage is the blending or uniting of individuals with two different natures into one. Therefore, it is important that both husband and wife are believers in Christ and have committed their self-centered natures to Him. This is a giant step toward having a happy, successful marriage. To reach oneness in Christ, it is imperative that each partner be filled with the Spirit and have a Christ-centered nature. And in marriage it is important to understand the temperaments and how through Christ the different temperaments can help you to strengthen your marriage: "But if we walk in the light as He is in the light, we have fellowship with one another, and the blood of Jesus Christ His Son cleanses us from all sin" (1 John 1:7).

OPPOSITES—BLESSING OR CURSE?

Most young lovers see only each other's strengths

before marriage. However, most of us are attracted to someone who has strengths in the area of our weaknesses. But then after marriage the weaknesses of our partners begin to appear. Marriage tends to pull the weaknesses to the surface. It is then a bride realizes that she did not marry the perfect man she thought she did!

If you had asked me when I first married what weaknesses my husband had that were sources of irritation to me, I could have written a chapter about it. But today, strange as it may seem, when I try to think back on those many things that, at the time, seemed to be driving a deep wedge between us, I find them very difficult to remember. The work of the Holy Spirit in our lives has melted our differences and weaknesses and has blended them together so we strengthen one another. We need each other. I need my husband's strengths and he needs mine. Together we can be a tower of strength as we face life's problems and as we do the work of the Lord because our lives are Spirit-filled.

My husband and I saw a wonderful example of two opposites strengthening each other once when he was asked to perform the wedding ceremony for a lovely young couple. The bride was about as pure sanguine as is possible, while the groom was thoroughly melancholic. The day of the wedding arrived, and one hour before the ceremony was to begin, the sanguine bride was joyfully parading up and down the aisles of the church, her gown and veil flowing as she passed out boutonnieres and bouquets. She was smiling radiantly and greeting everyone. This was her wedding day and she was enjoying it to the fullest extent!

ح▲ ——————————————————————

After marriage the weaknesses of
our partners begin to appear. Mar-
riage tends to pull the weaknesses
to the surface. It is then a bride
realizes that she did not marry the
perfect man she thought she did!

—————————————————————— ح▲

Meanwhile, my husband was in his study trying to hold up the melancholic groom, who was extremely nervous, and was wondering if anyone was coming to the wedding, if he had the ring, and even if the bride would be there on time. Little did he know what was really going on out in the sanctuary. The ceremony started and everything went beautifully until the time came for the couple to kneel at the altar while the soloist sang "The Lord's Prayer." Hearing a little commotion in front of him, my husband looked down and noticed that copious tears were running down the cheeks of the groom. The bride quickly sized up the situation, looked at my husband with a wink, and reached in her lace bridal gown neckline for a handkerchief to give to the groom. He wiped his eyes, handed it back to her, and just as the soloist sang the last note the bride tucked the damp handkerchief back in her bosom, smiling radiantly as though nothing had happened. They needed each other! For this was just the beginning of her ability to bring cheer into his life and perhaps even wipe away some tears. And he was sharing with her a very deep, sensitive nature that would enrich her life in years to come. Thank God for opposites!

BEAUTY OR THE BEAST

Many books have been written to women to encourage them in improving their outward appearance. I feel very strongly that when a woman fully accepts herself as a creation God has made, she will do her best to prune, trim, manicure, and even paint the object of God's love and care. It is a pity to see a Christian woman who has developed her inner beauty, but who has done nothing to the frame she must house it in. On the other hand, how beautiful is the woman who has obeyed the instructions in 1 Peter 3 to develop the hidden person of the heart and then has taken special care to trim and fix up the place in which it dwells.

Recently my husband and I were eating in a restaurant. Our meal was almost ruined when we overheard the man at the table across from us say to his wife, "You look like the devil. You look 85 years old. Why don't you spend five minutes putting on a little makeup and a wig?" This man was not right to run his wife down as he did. It was true—she did look dreadful, but there were plenty of other ways he could have lovingly communicated the same message. But that does not excuse his wife either. Who knows how many years he had been living with an unkempt wife? With all of the beauty-care products available today, there is no need for a woman to let herself get into this situation. Women don't have to be identified by plainness and a downtrodden appearance. God created all things beautiful. I'm sure He enjoys seeing a woman delight in taking care of His handiwork. God does want the hidden woman of the heart to be beautiful, but a little work on the outer woman helps the whole person. I believe it is God-honoring.

CONFLICT TO CONTENTMENT

With the blessing and enrichment of opposites comes the necessity for adjustment. The differences in a marriage do not need to lead to the divorce court or even be a threat to a marriage. When two people marry, there needs to be an agreement—a commitment for life—to make it work. The secret is really in how you handle the differences, for good marriages will survive any type of conflict. But those who survive serious conflicts are the marriages who have dealt with their problems prayerfully and are led by the Holy Spirit. As such, it is of utmost importance for wives to pray for their marriage in four different ways:

First of all, pray about your own attitude and response to the problem. When you examine your heart, you may find that you have some confessing to do. You cannot be filled with the Holy Spirit when you have wrong attitudes or emotions.

Secondly, pray for your husband even in times when you may not feel like praying for him. Nevertheless, ask God to help him to evaluate the situation and recognize his shortcomings.

Thirdly, ask God to lead you in discussing the

problem with your husband. You could ruin everything by discussing it in your own strength and in your own way.

And fourth, ask God to fill you with love for your husband so that you can genuinely love him regardless of your differences or his weaknesses. Many times this God-given love will cause the differences to melt away and fade into the past.

Not long after Tim and I married, I discovered one of his weaknesses that no one had warned me about. After a few days of wedded bliss, I detected a habit that would be repeated day after day. Each morning I would find my husband's socks right where he had removed his shoes the night before. They were never fully stretched out, but were always rolled up in little round balls—two of them! At first it was really no problem. I enjoyed picking up his socks, and since I had a strong back, it really didn't hurt me. But the days wore into weeks and the weeks into months. One morning I noticed a little irritation as I picked them up—an irritation not in my back, but in my attitude. A few days later I began to wonder who picked up after him before he met me. It then occurred to me that maybe he really didn't know that we had a clothes hamper. So I introduced him to this special piece of furniture built to hold dirty clothes. Nevertheless, I continued to stumble over the dirty socks each morning. Stumble? Yes, because they were growing in size—at least in my mind and attitude. "His back is certainly as strong as mine. He can pick up his own socks," I grumbled.

It is very interesting how something so small as

two dirty socks can throw your whole personality off balance. Just two socks irritated me so much that I became critical of many things that my husband did. Those socks sparked the fire that threw my mental attitude completely out of whack. When my husband would come home in the evening whistling or singing, I would not see the man who dearly loved me and provided for me. Instead, I would see the wearer of those dirty socks!

But one dull, gloomy day, I picked up the Bible by our nightstand and read a verse that seemed to stand out from all the other verses: "And whatever you do in word or deed, do all in the name of the Lord Jesus, giving thanks to God the Father through Him" (Colossians 3:17). In my own translation it seemed to say to me, "When you pick up after your husband, even his dirty socks, do it in the name of the Lord Jesus, giving thanks to God and the Father by Him." I quickly read on: "Wives, submit to your own husbands, as is fitting in the Lord" (verse 18).

My eyes dropped down a few verses: "And whatever you do, do it heartily, as to the Lord and not to men, knowing that from the Lord you will receive the reward of the inheritance; for you serve the Lord Christ" (verses 23,24).

I wasn't just picking up dirty socks for my husband; I was serving the Lord Jesus by doing this, so I had to do it heartily as unto Him. The Lord was using dirty socks to teach me a lesson.

I then faced a conflict. My husband may not have even known about it at the time. (However, I hardly think he hadn't noticed my rotten attitude.) Under examination, though, I was the one who had to confess and get my attitude straightened out. Interestingly enough, after I confessed, I truly enjoyed serving the Lord and my husband. It was almost a time of devotion each day as I lovingly picked up those blessed dirty socks. I thanked God for my loving husband who was so faithful, who provided for me, and who loved God with all his heart. I knew there were many women who would give anything to once again be able to pick up socks after their husbands. And I was still able!

But would you believe that those beautiful dirty socks began to disappear without any word spoken? One day he just decided to be more careful and to pick up after himself. Oh, how I missed those socks! But I still take them from the clothes hamper and put them into the washing machine. The Lord's lesson had been accomplished. So may I do it heartily as unto the Lord!

SHOULD WE HAVE CHILDREN?

With all of the birth-control methods and, sadly, even abortions that are available today, it is easily possible to go through life without choosing to have children. There was a day when only those who could not conceive did not have babies. The trend now is to have children only by choice, and even then they are scheduled. Some young couples even take a more sophisticated route, trying to help determine the sex of the baby before conception.

The day when every little girl had a baby doll to cuddle and to mother has swiftly passed. This may have begun when Barbie dolls with mature figures and clothes to match came on the scene. Then Ken arrived shortly after and began dating Barbie. Instead of little girls cuddling make-believe babies, they were living in a dream world of adults with Barbie and Ken. Recently one TV personality remarked that a popular doll manufacturer was producing Barbie and Ken dolls complete with sex organs. Little girls live these activities through their dolls and begin to think of themselves as sex partners instead of mothers.

Sex education in schools today rarely promotes the value of married love and parenting children after marriage. Motherhood for many girls is no longer a dream in the far-off future. Young unmarried girls are becoming mothers earlier and earlier. A baby of their own is someone to love who will love them. Marriage and motherhood have become very distorted. Confusion about marriage and parenting has caused them to be represented by some people as a burden that women should avoid. I hear some teenage girls say that they never want to have children because children are too much of a burden. I recall one lovely young lady who came to work for me at CWA. She had been a feminist before she came to Christ. During her years as an active member of the National Organization of Women, she determined that she never wanted to get married or to have children. Then one day she accepted God's love and His forgiveness for her. She later married a wonderful Christian man and came to work for me as my assistant. A few years went by and she was working through her attitude about children. God was at work in her life, and today she is a wonderful, loving mother of two beautiful children. I believe this is the normal desire that God puts in the hearts of women who love Him.

The point I am making is that with these changing times and attitudes, we have young married couples who decide they do not want to raise a family. I am not referring to temporary delays, but to permanent decisions. While not every couple must have children, I do feel that couples who do not pray about it to ascertain God's will may miss out on life's greatest blessing.

In all probability, the temperaments have a lot to do with these attitudes. Probably Sarah Sanguine would want to be a mother since she has so much love to give. She adores children anyway and would love to have her very own. Easygoing Polly Phlegmatic would be willing to go along with her husband's wishes and would be able to adjust to either having or not having children. Martha Melancholy would have a problem deciding if she could really be a good mother. She would want to experience mother-love before she ever conceived. And Clara Choleric might have such far-reaching goals that she feels a child would interfere with her success. At the very least, she would probably want a limit of one child. Each of these temperaments is influenced, of course, by her partner, so the decision might vary and be subject to change.

My husband and I were recently visiting with several young couples when, during the course of the evening, my husband asked about their children. I detected a few glances across the room and a little uneasiness. The subject was dropped for the moment but came to the surface again later. One of the uneasy wives remarked that she never wanted children. Another wife chimed in that she didn't either. My husband was not about to let that go, so he began to question their reasons. They both remarked that they felt they could not love a child sufficiently and so did not want children (both were melancholies). Their husbands would have enjoyed being fathers, but these wives were very firm. I commented that God gives a woman nine months of preparatory time. It is then that a mother's heart begins to learn to love the little life that is growing within her. The first movements, the increased measurements, the extra heartbeat all contribute to a mother's growing love for her unborn child. But these gals wanted to have that love before pregnancy. Melancholic women want to experience and be assured of mother-love before they ever conceive. But when pregnancy is approached with prayer and anticipation, a mother's heart will be filled with all the love she needs for her baby.

"Then God blessed them, and God said to them, 'Be fruitful and multiply; fill the earth'" (Genesis 1:28). The first commandment God gave to man was to multiply and replenish the earth. Today we have been deceived into thinking that the earth is overpopulated and that we can do our part by not having children. But that is only man's deception about overpopulation. It is God's wisdom that tells us to multiply. Our first responsibility is to be obedient to God who created all people and controls the destiny of the world in which we dwell.

As I talk to many childless couples, it soon becomes obvious that their true motives are not as noble as they seem on the surface. There is often a current of selfishness flowing beneath the most acceptable excuses. In order to be truly Spirit-controlled, young couples should not make such an important decision without first seeking what the heavenly Father would have them do. Blessing from God must be preceded by obedience.

DON'T BE AFRAID OF SUBMISSION

The woman who is truly Spirit-filled will want to be totally submissive to her husband. Contrary to what radical feminists advocate, submission does not mean that the wife who submits is a second-rate citizen. Submission is God's design for the wife just as the husband is assigned to be the head of the wife. The wife is to submit to the "headship" of the husband, not the "lordship." The husband is not the lord. Lordship is to coerce someone to follow your will, while headship is to be responsible for creating an environment of protection. Christ's example teaches that true submission is neither reluctant nor grudging, nor a result of imposed authority; rather, it is an act of obedience to God when it is a chosen, deliberate, voluntary response to a husband.

> . . . submitting to one another in the fear of God. Wives, submit to your own husbands, as to the Lord. For the husband is head of the wife, as also Christ is head of the church; and He is the Savior of the body. Therefore, just as the church is subject to Christ, so let the wives be to their own husbands in everything (Ephesians 5:21-24).

During Jesus' life on earth, He was in total submission to the Father and gave up every right He had. He did not lose His identity. On the contrary, He knew exactly who He was and for what purpose He was on earth—and He fulfilled that purpose. Even though He became a servant in human form, He knew that He was the Son of God, equal with God the Father. For in the Godhead there exists perfect unity, equality, and harmony.

Submission is not a status of inferiority. The husband is the head of the wife in the same way the Father is the head of Christ. They are equal and one, but there must be only one head. Yet a husband and wife are to function together as a team, complementing one another instead of competing with one another.

After I spoke at a women's luncheon, one little lady nearing her seventies came up to shake my hand. In a quivering voice she said, "Last week we celebrated our fiftieth wedding anniversary. For all of those years I have *let* my husband be the head of our home. Finally, about a week ago, I decided it was my turn and I took over. I have been acting as the head. We have been miserable for a whole week and both of us are irritable after 50 wonderful years. When you spoke today, I realized what our trouble was. I am not obeying God." I kissed her and told her to dry her tears. God saw that she was now willing to submit both in action and in attitude. Christ's example was not an attitude of unfairness felt toward the Father because Christ was the one chosen to become a servant. The Bible says He humbled himself and was obedient:

> Let this mind be in you which was also in Christ Jesus, who, being in the form of God, did not consider it robbery to be equal with

God, but made Himself of no reputation, taking the form of a servant, and coming in the likeness of men. And being found in appearance as a man, He humbled Himself and became obedient to the point of death, even the death of the cross (Philippians 2:5-8).

Verse 9 then goes on to say that God exalted Jesus and gave Him a name which was above every name.

Jesus was willing to be humbled, to be obedient unto death, and to be submissive. It is the principle of losing yourself to find yourself. As the wife humbles herself and submits to the headship of her husband, she will begin to find her real meaning in that relationship. By following God's principles, a woman can live fully by dying to her own ego and submitting to her husband.

Recently I had a business contact with a "well-liberated" woman. In the course of the conversation, she made a few remarks about her marriage before blurting, "I guess you know by now that I don't believe in being a clinging vine. The last thing I want is a husband who has to support me!" She described their unusual arrangement, since she seemed to feel that it needed an explanation. Her husband has his job and his own checking account, while she has her own position with her own account. They both contribute equal amounts to a joint fund for household expenses.

While this may sound great on the surface, underneath there was a steaming bed of coals ready to ignite into a flaming fire. It so happened that she was more successful than he was in the business world; consequently, she could afford a much nicer car than he. Her wardrobe was more elaborate, and she was going on a vacation alone this summer because he couldn't afford the kind of trip she could. Our conversation had almost come to a close when she finally said what I had already guessed: "I have lost respect for that man because he has not been more successful!"

> *When you have two individuals with two different sets of temperaments, there will naturally be differences of opinion. Conflicts will come, but commitment to work them out will keep a marriage together.*

If we could roll the calendar back a few years, I would dare to say that we could see why he was beaten down and unproductive. She had initiated this situation and was now sick and tired of the result. I am sure she had defined her rights and insisted on them, never considering working with him as a team and building each other up. I would guess that this husband was a phlegmatic and his wife a "liberated" choleric. In spite of their differences, the principles of God could have worked if she had been willing to submit. Now she is so liberated that the result is two lonely people going their solitary ways through life. I wonder what that man could have become if she had taken her strengths and humbly submitted herself to him, working with him and submitting to his headship.

The wife who truly loves her husband will make his happiness her primary goal. With this kind of motivation, they both are winners in the end.

Just because there is conflict or trouble in a marriage does not mean that you have to bail out. Divorce is not always the answer. When you have two individuals with two different sets of temperaments, there will naturally be differences of opinion. The stronger the temperaments, the stronger the conflicts. Conflicts will come, but commitment to work them out will keep a marriage together. It takes both partners allowing the Spirit to control their lives to live peaceably and happily. It has been our joy to watch many couples come to this decision in their marriage after much conflict and see how their lives and marriages have been transformed. With the help of the Holy Spirit, you can be married for keeps!

12

Temperaments and Communication

O ne of the easiest ways to diagnose temperament is through the examination of a person's speech patterns. Each person's style of speaking is usually a dead giveaway of his or her temperament. All four temperaments have their own speaking style. In fact, all 12 temperament blends have unique speaking styles.

Martha Melancholy (without the ministry of the Holy Spirit) is usually negative, critical, faultfinding, or disapproving. She finds it difficult to say something positive unless someone measures up to her perfectionist standard. Since that is impossible, instead she frequently criticizes her husband and children, never giving any encouragement. It is also characteristic of Martha to have a long memory of every mistake or error someone else has made, and a sadistic desire to bring it up. As women get older, they often tend to talk more. So unless Martha surrenders her speech to God and gains a Spirit-controlled tongue, she is usually very unpleasant to be around through the passing years.

In addition, she is unthankful by nature and often verbalizes her self-pitying thoughts. Self-pity brings on depression. By expressing self-pitying thoughts, Martha can easily make everyone else depressed. One reason some churches never go anywhere or do anything for God is because they have so many self-focused melancholies in leadership. The first hint of a good or progressive idea is then usually deluged by Martha Melancholy's depressive pessimism that immobilizes the Spirit. Unfortunately, many families function the same way.

As she becomes Spirit-filled, Martha Melancholy will first of all become thankful. Her motto and way of life will become 1 Thessalonians 5:18: "In everything give thanks; for this is the will of God in Christ Jesus concerning you." She will have to work at this all her life since it is contrary to her human nature, but with God's help she will become a source of praise and thanksgiving to her family and then to everyone around her. Nothing can transform a melancholy lady like thanksgiving living!

Martha will then become an encourager, telling her family she loves them and her children how happy she is that God sent them into her life. She will also begin to accept less than perfection in others (which makes it easier to accept it in herself and makes her a much happier person). And when she takes insult, injury, and rejection in stride, even praying for the perpetrator, Martha has really arrived spiritually.

Polly Phlegmatic is gentle and passive by natural temperament, and usually possesses a quiet spirit.

Consequently, her speech patterns are not too objectionable even at their worst. Frankly, Polly is a woman of few words. But if you listen carefully, her words will often give away the fear, worry, and selfishness in her heart. After all, the Bible injunction "out of the abundance of the heart the mouth speaks" is true of Polly. She has her own way of avoiding involvement and family activity. But fortunately for her, her humor often comes to her aid. If she is not careful, though, she can make a science of putting people down and humiliating them—all in a nice way, of course. In her own cautious way, Polly can be quite negative.

Spirit-filled Polly Phlegmatic, however, is given away by her speech. Instead of keeping her love for Christ and what he has done for her a great secret, Polly will seek opportunities to tell what great things God has done for her. Thus she will become more verbal than is her natural bent. True, she will never be the talking machine that other temperaments are. But when filled with the Spirit, Polly will no longer show her displeasure by long periods of silence. She will become more venturesome and giving of herself as she begins living by faith. And as she grows in her faith, she will see that God's promise to supply all our needs works for her, too. Her worries will subside while she becomes more outgoing and concerned for others. Gradually, Polly will find ways to reassure people of her love by verbalizing it voluntarily. She will then claim God's promise, "I can do all things through Christ who strengthens me."

Clara Choleric is afflicted with a razor-sharp, cruel, sarcastic, and cutting tongue. No one can cut a person to shreds and walk away as though they have done a great service for mankind or be more dictatorial than Clara. She usually intimidates people to give in to her way as she goes her active way through life with her tongue wagging, beating, cutting, and insulting. And when she gets angry—look out! That is why her children often grow up psychologically shell-shocked, insecure, and dying for approval. Most children of strong cholerics leave home early because it's a matter of survival. Her husband may clam up to keep the peace, but often leaves her for a woman who is easier to get along with, or at least one who will listen.

Many people say that women are not as given to profanity and dirty talk as men, but I would have to say (if my perception is true) that carnal choleric women may be the exception. They can make the air blue with their cursing. Hopefully, they will put off that former manner of conversation after they become Christians. But unless Clara is Spirit-filled, she can still be pretty condemning of others and their plans. Sometimes Clara will object to other people's plans, even if deep down she really likes them. She opposes things often simply because she did not originate the idea. One reason Clara Choleric's and Martha Melancholy's children may not grow up to serve the Lord is because their mothers, when not controlled by the Spirit, have "roast preacher" every Sunday for dinner. Christian parents who openly criticize their pastor in the home rarely raise kids who love and serve God.

Spirit-filled Clara Choleric is not only a miracle, but she is also a joy to be around. Gone are the verbal jabs that hurt and the carnal sarcasm. Instead, there is a genuine compassion and concern for others. Rather than interrupting others as they speak, Clara Choleric will actually listen to the opinions, feelings, and dreams of others. Encouraging words will come out of her mouth—ones that have what the Bible calls an edifying effect on others. Instead of criticizing almost every time she opens her mouth, Clara will use praise for others and their plans, even when she knows she could do something better. And instead of always bragging about herself and what she has done, she will make sure others receive her praise—her family, in particular. Once Clara begins to practice thanksgiving and learns God's will for her life, thanksgiving will be almost as great a blessing to Clara as it is to Martha Melancholy. And you know Clara has arrived when she publicly admits how insensitive she has been in the past or, even more, when she apologizes for all the hurts and emotional wounds she has caused. Clara Choleric can be a good leader of the work of God if she learns to submit to Him and her church's authority, and if she learns to overcome her anger—which could be her greatest spiritual test.

Sarah Sanguine is often known by her tongue. It is like a machine gun wide open. And since Sarah is her favorite person, her endless stories and chatter revolve around herself. She flits in conversation even faster than she does in life. Silence is a threat to her that must be filled. Many times she starts talking even before she knows what she wants to say. I have heard many sanguines change course in the middle of a conversation and pretend that it is what they meant to say all the time. Sarah often interrupts people with abandon and thinks nothing of humiliating others by correcting them dogmatically, even when they aren't wrong.

She will usually say whatever it takes to attract attention, whether it be shocking, an exaggeration, or an outright lie. In fact, Sarah Sanguine learns early in life that exaggerating the truth makes her stories much more interesting, which gains her more attention and a larger audience. Although Sarah doesn't like to hurt people with her tongue deliberately, she will if she needs to protect herself. And when she gets angry, few people can hurt others with their tongue better than Sarah. She is often given to loose and foolish jesting, while her conversation can go from suggestive to dirty. It's dangerous to laugh at Sarah's shady speech, for it will only encourage her. Frequently, Sarah Sanguine can give pious speeches at church or at a Christian women's club—even though some know she isn't living what she is speaking. No one needs the biblical injunction more to "study to be quiet" than Sarah Sanguine.

However, Spirit-filled Sarah Sanguine can be a delight to be around. Her speech is not only cleaned up, but it also glorifies God rather than herself. And although she will always be a conversationalist, she will tend to steer the conversation in the direction of what great things the Lord has done. No one can be lastingly filled with the Spirit without reading the Word of God regularly. When Spirit-filled, Sarah will have something meaningful to say to others at church or in other Christian groups. She will study before teaching her Bible class rather than just winging it. When filled with the Spirit, Sarah's natural charisma will draw others to Christ. No one has the gift of evangelism like Spirit-filled Sarah. And she can reach out in compassion to others, beginning with the members of her own household. Sanguines are more people-oriented than other temperaments. And when filled with the Spirit, her concern is that others will come into a right relationship to God through His Son, Jesus. The church has benefited much by the enthusiastic service of sanguine temperaments, but as is true of all the temperaments, only when they are controlled by the Holy Spirit.

ANGER DESTROYS LOVE, COMMUNICATION, AND MARRIAGE

Most experienced marriage counselors say that lack of communication is the major cause of our nation's catastrophic divorce rate, which has hovered at about 51 percent for several years. My husband, who has counseled thousands of married people, disagrees however. He is convinced that a lack of communication or bad communication is caused by a lack of love or the death of love. And since no couples get married without at least thinking they are in love, we need to ask, "What causes love to die?" The best answer is, "Anger." And while we will deal pointedly with anger later in this book, I will say now that anger will always kill love eventually. If two lovers face differences of opinion, background, desires, and temperament with anger, then love is the casualty. This is what usually happens with selfish people. Our gift of speech then becomes a way of communicating anger despite the hurt and pain we have all felt when spoken to in anger by the one we love. Even those who suffer in silence eventually will snap and, as a result, love dies.

> *The Bible wisely points out, "Let all bitterness, wrath, anger, clamor, and evil speaking be put away from you. . . . Be kind to one another, tenderhearted, forgiving. . . ."*

One of the reasons divorce is so painful is that, long before a couple sees the lawyer, they have cut and hurt each other with their cruelest weapon: the tongue. And when most people get angry enough, they resort to hurtful and abusive words. Some even resort to physical violence, but that usually follows abusive speech. Each time cruel and unkind speech is hurled at the one we love, their love dies a little, until eventually it is dead—killed by the one instrument that first ignited that love: the tongue.

The Bible wisely points out to married couples, "And do not grieve the Holy Spirit of God. . . . Let all bitterness, wrath, anger, clamor, and evil speaking be put away from you, with all malice [enmity of heart]. And be kind to one another, tenderhearted, forgiving one another, just as God in Christ also forgave you" (Ephesians 4:30-32).

I really believe there is hope for any marriage if a couple will apply those verses above. It takes God's help through His Holy Spirit, but it can be done. We have seen many "impossible" cases restored to love and happiness, but never if angry, hurtful words are not . . .

1. forgiven

2. anger put off

3. evil speaking discontinued

4. tenderness and kindness restored

5. corrupt communication no longer allowed to proceed out of their mouths and

6. their mouths used to communicate that which is good to the use of edifying, that it may minister grace to the hearers.

Couples who use the unique, God-given gift that only we humans enjoy, the gift of communication, to edify and bring grace to each other do live happily ever after. That doesn't mean they don't have differences, for we all do. But their love-motivated communication enables them to resolve their differences. And when anger is removed, love flourishes. That's the way we are made, regardless of temperament. If you and your mate are not happy with your present means of communicating, do what we have assigned thousands of couples in the counseling room to do. Memorize Ephesians 4:29-32, and incorporate these principles into your marriage. Everyone wants love. That is why we get married—because we want someone to whom we can give love and from whom we can receive love. Communication, over the long years of a lifetime, is even more powerful than sex as a way of sharing that love.

The art of communicating does not mean one person must be an excessive talker. Communicating involves listening as well as talking. One dear, talkative lady seriously said to me, "I have no trouble communicating," but the truth was that she was dead wrong. What she really should have said was, "I have no trouble talking." She did all of the talking. Her husband was rarely able to express his views. She knew exactly what she thought, but did not listen to her husband's ideas. He was a great guy. I can just imagine what a wealth of thoughts he had stored up in his mind that he was not allowed to spill out.

Communicating is a two-way street. It must involve listening as well as talking. The lack of proper communication is one of the greatest problems in marriages today. Women need to pray for a Spirit-controlled tongue to know when to keep silent and when to speak, as well as how to say what must be said. How we say something is just as important as what we say.

One of the main ingredients in good communication is love. First Corinthians 13 lists many good qualities, but without love, these qualities are nothing. When the description of love in this chapter is used in a marriage, the line of communication between husband and wife will greatly improve. This is truly Spirit-filled communicating.

Love . . . suffereth long.
Love . . . is kind.
Love . . . envieth not.
Love . . . vaunteth not itself.
Love . . . is not puffed up.
Love . . . does not behave itself unseemly.
Love . . . seeketh not her own.
Love . . . is not easily provoked.
Love . . . thinketh not evil.

Love . . . rejoiceth not in iniquity.
Love . . . rejoiceth in the truth.
Love . . . beareth all things.
Love . . . believeth all things.
Love . . . hopeth all things.
Love . . . endureth all things.
Love . . . never faileth.

This love, or communication, is not dependent on the way your husband treats you. It becomes your responsibility to treat him this way. When you accept this responsibility, the line of communication will be wide open for you.

I would like to insert a thought right here that has been shared by many men. Most wives do not realize how easily their remarks can influence the thinking of their husbands. Often just a quick complaint, a criticism, or a negative remark can color the thoughts of a man. One minister-husband remarked that he never allowed his wife to speak a negative remark to him regarding any member of their church. Such a remark so influenced his thoughts toward that person that he was not able to shake it off. The Bible speaks quite clearly about this: "Do not speak evil of one another, brethren. He who speaks evil of a brother and judges his brother, speaks evil of the law and judges the law. But if you judge the law, you are not a doer of the law but a judge" (James 4:11).

There have been times when I have carelessly made a comment about someone to my husband. Unknowingly, that remark stuck in the files of his mind, eventually influencing him for good or bad regarding that person. The Spirit-filled woman must guard her thoughts and remarks lest she bring unnecessary judgment on another individual. We are guilty of praising God one moment and then bringing destruction to someone the next: "With it we bless our God and Father, and with it we curse men, who have been made in the similitude of God. Out of the same mouth proceed blessing and cursing. My brethren, these things ought not to be so" (James 3:9,10).

I have learned that on some occasions it is better for me to communicate with God about a matter and let Him speak to my husband.

The Holy Spirit can put controls on our tongues so that our communications may be wise and flavored with love. James goes on to say that from the wise only good deeds and comments will pour forth, and that if we don't brag about them, then we will be truly wise.

I have learned that on some occasions it is better for me to communicate with God about a matter and let Him speak to my husband. There are a few subjects that I seem to really mess up when I try to interfere.

Several few years ago we were traveling in Europe with two of our children. This was a testing time at best, since we were usually crammed together for many hours a day in a hotel, car, or train. Looking for ways to make the trip enjoyable for everyone, I was concerned that we were omitting an important matter from our fellowship. In the excitement of traveling—with passports, trains, foreign languages, and all the rest—we had neglected to pray together as a family. There were days when I would hint, nag, or even announce that we were struggling because we had not prayed. Then I decided that it would be far more effective and meaningful to the family if my husband would initiate the idea. So I committed it to the Lord, although I didn't really expect much to happen. You can imagine how surprised I was then when somewhere between Vienna and Innsbruck my husband stopped the car and said, "Family, we've been neglecting to have prayer together, and we should not go any further without praying!" What a beautiful, sweet spirit of prayer we had, and how thankful I was that I had not manipulated it. God had communicated for me!

Proper communication, then, must contain love and wisdom guided by the Holy Spirit. The harvest that you reap will be an honest, peaceable sharing of two hearts and minds.

"But the wisdom that is from above is first pure, then peaceable, gentle, willing to yield, full of mercy and good fruits, without partiality and without hypocrisy. Now the fruit of righteousness is sown in peace by those who make peace" (James 3:17,18).

13

Temperaments and Your Love Life

*T*he single most powerful influence on anyone's behavior, humanly speaking, is his or her temperament. Although background, childhood training, education, environment, and a host of other factors make an impression on us, nothing is more significant than the temperament traits we inherit at birth, for they produce our actions, reactions, and motivations. Training can make a shy woman more outgoing, but she will never become a comfortable extrovert. Education will discipline the dynamic, aggressive individual, but it will never transform her into Minnie Mouse. People are born either extroverts or introverts because these characteristics are an outgrowth of their temperament.

Since temperament has such an influence on a person's behavior, it follows that it will have a profound effect on another very powerful human instinct: the sex drive. In fact, a couple's intimate bedroom responses will often be a reflection of their temperaments. Although most Christians seldom relate the Holy Spirit to lovemaking in marriage, you will find that a person's relationship with God does influence this intimate area of marriage. As my husband and I explained in our book *The Act of Marriage* (Zondervan Publishing House, 1976), we are convinced that Christians who are properly motivated by the Spirit enjoy a better married love life than anyone else in today's society. Our detailed sex survey, taken from 1700 couples, revealed that Christians not only scored ten points higher in satisfaction in this area than non-Christians, but also that Spirit-filled Christians registered seven points higher than non-Spirit-controlled Christians.

> *A couple's intimate responses will often be a reflection of their temperaments.*

Since lovemaking involves both the husband and the wife, let's examine each of the four temperaments in both sexes to demonstrate how they are most likely to respond sexually. We will first consider responses, appetites, hang-ups, and basic needs. Then I will offer some suggestions for wives on how to become the kind of marriage partner that God created them to be.

The Sanguine Husband

Sam Sanguine is so responsive that it doesn't take

much to turn him on. And since he is so obvious about everything he does, his wife is instantly aware of his mood. A natural charmer, Sam thinks he can turn the head of a female marble statue with his flattery. And he usually can—unless he is married to her. Sam has a great appetite for everything, including lovemaking.

Most sanguines have very few hang-ups about sex and usually make it clear that they enjoy it. If it isn't the most important thing in life for them, it's a close second. The sanguine husband is usually reluctant to take "no" for an answer. In fact, he can easily be hurt or deflated if his wife does not respond to his gestures of love. He may outwardly project the idea that he is God's gift to women, but underneath he has a great need for affection. If he is not satisfied at home, Sam, more than any other temperament, may seek affection elsewhere for two reasons: 1) the conquest of another woman is necessary to satisfy his powerful ego, and he finds lonely, unfulfilled women easy prey to his charm; and 2) he is weak-willed and emotionally excitable. Consequently, he is vulnerable to the unscrupulous woman.

Sam Sanguine's needs. The supersex emphasis of our day is very hard on Sam, for he is easily stimulated. He has four basic needs in this area:

1. Moral principles deeply ingrained in his heart and mind from childhood that show God's plan of one man for one woman "so long as they both shall live."

2. The concept of walking in the Spirit, particularly in his thought life. Romans 13:14 says,

"Make no provision [forethought] for the flesh, to fulfill its lusts." If a sanguine indulges in immoral fantasies, he will soon fan his passions out of control and will commit the sin of adultery to the heartache of his wife and himself. Once the moral barrier is broken, it is easy for him to repeat his sin.

3. A loving, responsive, affectionate wife who freely lets her husband know how much she enjoys his love. Husbands treated like that rarely stray, regardless of their temperament.

4. A wife who becomes the *sole* object of his exuberant affection. He must avoid the flirtations and flattery of other women (thereby reassuring both his own wife and other women's husbands). Also, he should concentrate on bringing joy and fulfillment to his wife.

THE SANGUINE WIFE

There are very few differences in sexual response that distinguish a sanguine man from a sanguine woman. Sarah Sanguine is a cheerful, happy, affectionate cheerleader-type who has the gift of making men feel comfortable in her presence. Her charming personality makes her a hit with all types of men, and in her naiveté she can turn them on without realizing it. She usually thinks she is just being friendly.

As a wife, Sarah has a tremendous amount of love to impart to her husband and family. Lovemaking is very important to her, and it doesn't usually take too much coaxing to get her into the mood. Even if hurt or angry, she rather easily can moderate her attitude. Sanguines rarely carry a grudge—a trait essential for any marriage! And she is the most likely type to greet her husband at the door to give him a "kiss with a future." Of all the temperaments, she is the one most likely to jolt her husband after reading *The Total Woman* by meeting him at the door dressed only in boots and an apron. Since she rarely has hang-ups about anything, she usually maintains a good attitude toward sex, often in spite of disastrously distorted misconceptions that may have been handed down from her mother. Her natural ability to express herself helps Sarah overcome her inhibitions, and she quickly finds that she can heighten her lovemaking enjoyment by being aggressive. Unless unwisely stifled by her husband, Sarah will usually learn early on that passivity in lovemaking is not for her. Her sanguine moodswings vary, bringing great delight to her partner. These wives have a tremendous desire to please their partners. And with a reasonable amount of encouragement and cooperation, they usually succeed in this area of marriage, provided their shortcomings in other areas do not become their partner's obsessions.

Sarah Sanguine's needs. The fun-loving Sarah Sanguine starts out in marriage expecting to enjoy it. The following suggestions will help her to realize that potential:

1. Cultivate a strong spiritual life by walking in the Spirit, regularly studying the Word of God, and obeying His standards of moral behavior.

2. Recognize her ability to excite men other than her husband and avoid any flirtations that would provoke his jealousy or confront her with temptations.

3. Soften her extroversion so she will not embarrass her husband. It is especially important to learn that a loud, overbubbly wife may gain the attention of other men, but disapproval from her husband.

4. Dearly love a mate who will assure her of his approval and acceptance and give her tender words of encouragement, attention, and affection. If she receives these, she will give attention to proper grooming, fashion, manners, good housekeeping, and whatever else will make her pleasing to her husband.

THE CHOLERIC HUSBAND

On the surface, Carl Choleric as a suitor appears to be a great lover. Candy and flowers in abundance, politeness, kindness, and dynamic leadership make him appear to be the embodiment of manliness. But somehow that tends to change shortly after marriage. Carl Choleric is so goal-conscious that he is willing to do almost anything to attain his desires. Since the "special lady in his life" is subconsciously a goal before marriage, Carl is willing to pay any price to win her hand. Once married, however, the goal is changed. Now he wants to support her properly. Consequently, he may work from 12 to 20 hours a day. The hardest thing for Carl Choleric to understand is that his wife did not marry him for what he could give her, but rather for himself. When confronted with his wife's complaint that he doesn't love her anymore, Carl is likely to respond, "Of course I love you; I work like a slave to give you what you want." But the truth of the matter is, he enjoys work.

Emotionally, Carl Choleric is an extremist; he is either hot or cold. He can get furiously angry and explode over anything, much to the horror of his new bride when she first experiences these outbursts. Carl's impatience and inability to lavish affection on her may make adjustment difficult for her. Showing affection is just "not his thing." One woman once said about her choleric husband, "Kissing my husband is like kissing a marble statue in the cemetery on a winter day."

Carl Choleric's impetuous traits likewise hinder his proper adjustment to marriage. Just as he is apt to set out on a trip before consulting a road map, he is prone to take his wife to the bedroom without the slightest sex education himself. Somehow he thinks it will all work out!

Fortunately, Carl Choleric does possess one important trait that helps his love life: his practical nature. Once Carl realizes that lovemaking involves more than preparing for a 100-yard dash—that he must be tender, gentle, affectionate, thoughtful, and sensitive to his wife's needs—he learns quickly. In the learning process he will usually find that affection is exciting and that watching the woman he loves respond to his touch is extremely fulfilling.

Carl Choleric's needs. The most underdeveloped part of a choleric is his emotional life. And since lovemaking at its best is motivated by emotion, he has many needs:

1. To show love and compassion for others. Nothing short of the personal experience of receiving Christ as Lord and Savior and learning to walk in the Spirit will provide Carl Choleric with this ability. Even after his conversion, it often takes some time before the love of God will characterize his life.

2. To understand that many people are not as self-sufficient as he. Even though they may be as capable, they will not be as confident that they can perform well. Carl must realize that other people may tend to harbor doubts much more easily than he. If he will patiently show kindness and encourage his wife, she will be a better performer.

3. To develop tenderness and affection for his wife and children and to voice his approval and commendation of them. He must learn to say "I love you" quite frequently to his wife and show his pride in her. Because the choleric is a natural leader, people tend to look to him for approval, love, and acceptance. He can cause them to wither with a disappointing look and condemning word, or he can lift their spirits by going out of his way to approve and commend them. Those who have been rejected by Carl may tend to build a shell

around their egos in order to protect themselves and to ward off future injuries. When Carl Choleric the father and husband becomes sensitive to the emotional needs of his family, he can even spark emotions within himself that would otherwise remain dormant. To say "I love you" to his wife is not easy, but when he forgets himself, recognizes the importance of these words to his loved one, and concentrates on her emotional well-being, Carl will learn quickly—and he will thoroughly enjoy the response it brings.

4. To eliminate sarcasm and disrespectful speech from his vocabulary. Unkind and resentful words never turn a wife on!

5. To learn to overcome his inner hostilities and anger for two reasons: First, "grieving the Spirit" through anger (Ephesians 4:30-32) will keep him a spiritual pygmy all of his Christian life; and second, the threat of an instant choleric explosion inhibits the emotional expressions of his wife. It is difficult for a choleric Christian to realize that his spiritual life will affect his bedroom life, but it does—one way or the other.

The Choleric Wife

Clara Choleric is usually an exciting creature, particularly if one does not have to live with her. She is extremely active in every area of life—a dynamic, forceful individual with multiple goals in mind. At the same time she may feature a spitfire personality and a razor-blade tongue, which dominates and controls every activity in which she is involved.

In my late teens there was such a girl in our youth group. Many guys dated her because she was fun to be with, but they kiddingly remarked behind her back, "Don't marry Evelyn unless you want to be president of the United States."

The necessity of having a positive mental attitude toward lovemaking in marriage comes into focus when dealing with Clara Choleric as a wife. If she observed a warm, loving relationship between her parents while she was growing up, Clara will probably enter marriage expecting to enjoy lovemaking. Cholerics usually achieve what they set out to do, and she will probably not be disappointed—nor will her husband.

On the other hand, if Clara has been raised by unhappy, bickering parents, has been molested, or has endured other traumatic experiences in childhood—or even if she was taught that "sex is dirty" for either religious or other ill-conceived reasons—she may encounter serious difficulty in relating properly to her husband. Clara Choleric is so opinionated that once obsessed with the idea that "sex is not for nice girls," she might even reject the angel Gabriel carrying a message on a stone tablet saying, "Marriage is honorable among all." But once convinced that God wants her to enjoy sex, Clara can usually make a quick transition to a happy love life.

Choleric wives often acquire several potential hang-ups in this department. They are not usually given to open affection, and thus they often stifle their husband's advances before their own motor rolls into action. In addition, if not Spirit-filled, Clara Choleric tends to demasculinize a man by dominating and leading him in everything—including sex. It takes a Spirit-led, thoughtful choleric woman to recognize that she ignores her husband's ego at her own peril.

We have observed that opposites attract each other in marriage; consequently, a choleric woman will usually select a passive partner. If she isn't especially fond of lovemaking, she and her husband may go for long periods without it because he may be too passive to say or do anything about it. But whether or not he raises the issue, you can be sure he doesn't enjoy the abstinence! Ultimately, an explosion usually occurs—and almost always with serious consequences.

It is to the choleric wife's credit, however, that she will usually adjust and become a very enjoyable partner once she learns how important a good bedroom life is to her husband. She needs to realize that the success of her marriage may well depend upon her willingness to let her husband maintain leadership in this intimate area of their lives.

Clara Choleric's needs. Like her male counterpart, Clara Choleric has many needs. These are some of the most important for her to consider:

1. To walk in the Spirit in order to conquer her hot temper and sarcastic tongue and to develop her emotional capability to show love and affection. Being loving and affectionate is certainly easier for some temperaments than others, but God would never have commanded

that we love one another if He had not made it possible for all of us. Cholerics may need to work at it a little harder than some, but the more they express love, the easier it will come.

2. To learn forgiveness—especially for her father, if necessary. No woman can fully enjoy her husband if she harbors hatred or anger toward her father. This is especially true of strong-minded, opinionated, willful cholerics. They will vent their frustrated wrath on their husbands, and stifle their expressions of love. A choleric woman may have this problem because she resisted her father's affections as a little girl. Because her father did not understand, he may have closed her out of his heart and had little to do with her—simply because he did not know how to reach her. Not realizing why she was rejected by her daddy, the choleric girl may then increasingly withdraw from him and refuse to show any normal expressions of emotion toward him—all the while fostering a growing resentment toward men.

3. To avoid heaping sarcasm, criticism, and ridicule on her husband, particularly in the lovemaking area. Cholerics exude so much self-confidence that, even without saying anything, they cause others to feel inadequate. The choleric woman needs to let her husband know how much she values him as a man and

a lover. No compliment is sweeter and cherished longer than one which expresses appreciation for the masculinity or femininity of one's spouse.

4. To take time to express love to her husband. Cholerics are often night people. Early-bird husbands may crawl into bed at 10 or 11 o'clock, hoping for a little tenderness and love, but then fall asleep while their choleric wives finish a book, clean the house, or pursue countless other activities which their active minds suggest. Many choleric wives could improve their love lives just by going to bed earlier.

5. To learn submission by biblical standards. A choleric likes to lead and usually makes a good leader, but by the grace of God and in obedience to His Word, such a wife needs to bring herself into submission to her husband. If she attempts to assume the husband's role and responsibilities in the home, she is courting disaster. A passive husband will give his wife more love, respect, and flexibility if she encourages him to take the responsibility and leadership of their home.

THE MELANCHOLY HUSBAND

Marvin Melancholy is a supreme idealist. He usually goes into marriage without any sex education because he idealistically believes that everything will work out. If he is blessed with an amorous and exciting wife who has no hang-ups, everything usually does work out. But if Marvin marries someone as naive as he, he and his wife may come home from their honeymoon depressed. When the love life of a couple is deficient, it can create a shaky experience for a melancholic husband. His wife will especially be turned off by his depression, and this will further complicate matters. But it is usually quite difficult for Marvin to seek counseling until his marriage enters a precarious phase.

Marvin Melancholy has the capacity to express true love more than any other temperament. He is a loyal and faithful partner unless he indulges in impure thoughts and becomes involved in promiscuity. But when Marvin Melancholy loves his wife, he will almost overextend himself in thoughtfulness, kindness, and emotion.

Among Marvin Melancholy's greatest assets is his romantic nature. So he does all of those things that delight the romantic heart of a woman: soft music, dim lights, perfume.

And because he is extremely analytical, Martin will quickly learn what his wife finds pleasurable and then will enjoy bringing her to fulfillment. If everything goes well for them, this couple can become great lovers.

Unfortunately, everything in life doesn't always turn out perfectly, and marriage is no exception. Melancholies are such perfectionists that they almost refuse to accept anything less than perfection. Many a melancholic man can come home all "revved up" for his wife, only to have his ardor cooled by dirty dishes in the sink or the kids' toys in the middle of the floor. In fact, I know one melancholic husband who could be turned on by watching his wife get undressed for bed and turned off because she didn't hang up her clothes. At a time like that, a sanguine or choleric wouldn't even notice the clothes!

The sensitive traits of the melancholic, that on most occasions make him aware of his wife's needs for tenderness and love, may also work against him at times. He is prone to interpret his wife's lack of immediate response when he first initiates lovemaking as rejection. And if his wife is in a coy mood (as many women frequently are) and wants mild pursuit, he is apt to think she doesn't desire him and to give up before she can reveal her true feelings.

Marvin Melancholy's needs. The melancholic individual has a tremendous amount of love to give to others if granted the slightest encouragement. These are some of his most obvious needs:

1. Maintaining a vital, personal relationship with God and a daily Spirit-filled experience that keeps him "other-oriented" instead of obsessed with himself. No selfish or self-centered person will be a good lover, no matter what his temperament. The real evidence of when a melancholic is walking in the Spirit appears when he breaks that self-centered syndrome.

2. Learning to give unconditional love, not rewarded love. A wife once told me that her husband was a natural nitpicker. "He has a long checklist for housekeeping, and if I don't

rate an 'A' before we go to bed, he will not make love to me," she complained.

3. Avoiding a critical and pessimistic attitude, which are two of the biggest problems of a melancholic. Because of his perfectionism, the melancholic husband often expects unrealistic standards of achievement for himself and others. This in turn causes him to become frequently disillusioned when things and people don't measure up.

4. Maintaining a positive and wholesome thought life (Philippians 4:8). He should never indulge in revengeful thought patterns or self-pity. Instead he should always "give thanks in everything" (1 Thessalonians 5:18).

5. Marrying a woman who is not easily offended and can cheerfully encourage him when he is down, reassure him of his manhood when he is insecure, and take his criticism lightly. As long as she knows he is moody, she can patiently wait a little while for his mood to change.

6. Concentrating on God and thanking Him for his wife's strengths. He must regularly encourage her with verbal assurances of love and approval. I have seen many sanguine wives go through a personality change under the constant criticism of a melancholic husband. Unfortunately, when he is finished, even Marvin Melancholy doesn't like his creation.

THE MELANCHOLY WIFE

Martha Melancholy is an unpredictable love partner, for she has the greatest of all mood swings. On some occasions she can be as exciting and stimulating as any sanguine. On others she has absolutely no interest in anything—including love. She may meet her husband at the door and sweep him off his feet right into the bedroom, or she may ignore his arrival completely.

Martha Melancholy is the supreme romantic, and her moods are as apparent as the noonday sun. When in the mood for love, she resorts to dinner by candlelight, soft music, and heavy perfume. (If she's married to a sanguine, that works quite well; but if her husband is a choleric, she may be in trouble, because he often detests perfume.)

Although she has the capability of enjoying ecstatic love at heights that would choke other temperaments, Martha is rarely interested in setting world records for frequency. To her, quality is always preferable to quantity. Of all the temperament types, she is the most apt to engage in bedroom roulette—that is, she dispenses love as a reward for good behavior. However, no man worthy of the title will put up with that!

Martha Melancholy is often plagued with excessive prudishness, especially if her mother had a problem in this area. She may use trumped-up religious arguments to excuse her sexual abstinence; her real problem, however, probably stems from her premarital resolution that sex is undesirable. As a result, she never gives herself the opportunity to learn otherwise. Martha is the type who saves lovemaking only for propagation, never for pleasure. A study of the Scriptures can teach her differently.

Little things can quickly be turned into huge problems for Martha Melancholy. Her husband's inability to balance the checkbook, his forgetting to run an errand, or his neglecting to bathe may thoroughly upset her and send her into quiet revenge. She feels that if he didn't keep his part of a bargain, she doesn't need to keep hers—and thus she refrains from lovemaking. What she doesn't realize is that she is cheating herself out of both the enjoyment of lovemaking and the loving approval of her husband.

I counseled a melancholic wife who had not made love with her husband for several weeks. She was only interested at night, but by the time she was ready for bed, he had collapsed. She complained, "He goes to bed tired, and he never even takes time to bathe or brush his teeth. In the morning I am a zombie and he is charged up. But I can't stand his body smell and bad breath then!" I suggested that she learn to accept her husband and not try to change him. This was hard medicine for a wife to take, but before long she discovered that by cooperating with him, he was quite willing to modify his habits for her.

Another hang-up common to Martha Melancholy is jealousy. Not given to "insincere flirtation," Martha often marries a man who is outgoing and friendly to everyone. It is not uncommon for her to ride home in icy silence after a party because her husband flirted with every woman there. Since her husband's male ego gets so little food at home, he unwisely seeks it at social gatherings. And he may often think, "Nothing I do ever satisfies that woman."

Seated across from the beautiful wife of a wealthy and dynamic Christian businessman, I was startled to hear his melancholic wife ask me, "Would you explain why I am so jealous of my husband even when I know I have no reason for it?" It seems that he had dismissed three successive secretaries and finally hired the homeliest gal he could find because of his wife's jealousy. But it still didn't solve her problem. I responded, "The problem is not with your husband; you just don't like yourself." Tears ran down her checks as she admitted to strong feelings of self-rejection. Later, her husband commented on their love life: "When her groundless suspicions make her jealous, I can't touch her. But when she is sorry for her accusations, she can't get enough of me. I never know whether to expect feast or famine!"

Martha's biggest problem in life will be her tendency toward self-pity. A melancholic can follow the slightest insult or rejection with self-pitying thoughts that plunge her into a state of depression until she is not interested in love or anything else.

Martha Melancholy's needs. The emotional capability of a melancholic is so extensive that she has the potential of being an exciting and fulfilling love partner if her weaknesses don't overpower her strengths. Here are some of her specific needs:

1. A vital and effective relationship with Jesus Christ, walking in His Spirit, so that she may enjoy the love, peace, and joy He gives to make her an effective person.

2. A thankful attitude for all of the blessings God has given her, instead of thinking or verbalizing criticism for the things that don't please her. She will discover that a positive mental attitude combined with thanksgiving can give her a happier outlook on life and make her a more pleasant person for others to be around. This attitude will also help her to accept herself as she is, for self-condemnation will destroy her. It is very difficult for people to like her if she does not like herself.

3. Acceptance of her husband as he is, permitting God to make any changes that are needed. Her submission to him should not be dependent on his behavior, but on her obedience to God.

4. Encouragement and reassurances of love from her husband. A thoughtful and verbally expressive husband who proves his love in many other areas of their marriage will be rewarded in this one.

5. The request that God give her an unconditional love for her husband and the ability to love him to the point that she forgets about herself. She needs to realize that married love is beautiful because it is God's plan for married partners. Our Lord promises that a woman who gives herself without reservation to her husband will be loved. He said, "Give and it shall be given unto you," and "Whatsoever a man soweth, that shall he also reap." If a

woman sows love, she will surely reap it in abundance.

6. The lesson of forgiveness. Almost every durable marriage requires forgiveness along the way. Because an unforgiving attitude will always destroy a relationship, a married couple must realize that because God commands it, their harmony requires forgiveness (Matthew 18:35; Mark 11:25).

THE PHLEGMATIC HUSBAND

Not much is known about the bedroom life of Philip Phlegmatic. He is without doubt the world's most closemouthed individual, particularly concerning his personal life. What is known about this intimate area usually comes from an irate partner; consequently, the information could well be biased. In fairness to the phlegmatic male, therefore, any suggestions we make concerning his lovemaking responses must be evaluated on the basis of deductive analysis and hearsay reporting.

Some assume that because Philip Phlegmatic is easygoing and prone to be unmotivated, he may not be a very spirited lover. But that may not always be true. If a study of the habits of phlegmatics is indicative, we find that they usually accomplish more than they are given credit for. They just don't make noise and attract much attention to their achievements as do other temperaments. Rather, they make good use of their expended efforts. When Philip Phlegmatic wants to do something, he follows through effectively and promptly in his own quiet way. We suspect that is also the way he makes love.

One characteristic of phlegmatics should help their love life: their abundant kindness. Rarely, if ever, would Philip Phlegmatic embarrass or insult his wife; sarcasm is just not his way. Philip should have little trouble gaining love from his wife because women usually respond to a man who is kind to them.

Another advantageous trait in Philip Phlegmatic is that he rarely gets angry and very seldom creates irritation in others. If his fiery wife screams at him for some reason, Philip's response usually extinguishes her fire because he is a master of the soft answer. Consequently, the storm has usually passed by bedtime, and he can conveniently act as if the incident never happened.

Phlegmatic men often have a way of getting things to go their way by waiting for them. They are patience personified, apparently able to outwait others. Their love life is probably like that. As the intensity of their youthful sex drive cools down somewhat, phlegmatic husbands patiently teach their wives to originate lovemaking. If the truth were known, they probably get all the love they want in marriage, perhaps even more frequently and better than some of the more tempestuous types. They are simply more prone than other temperaments to let their wives initiate lovemaking.

Three areas may cause Philip Phlegmatic serious trouble, however. First, he tends to be reluctant to assert himself and take leadership unless it is thrust upon him. But when he does lead, Philip performs his tasks admirably. However, when he fails to take the leadership in the home, his wife can become very disillusioned. The wife who expects such a husband to assume the initiative in the bedroom may soon feel unloved. Sometimes she loses respect for her phlegmatic husband because he doesn't seem to assert his manhood.

A second danger spot is Philip Phlegmatic's selfishness, which makes him stingy, stubborn (in a polite way), and self-indulgent. Yielding to these weaknesses can produce resentment in a wife, such as when her husband never takes her out. As we have already seen, resentment stifles love.

The third potential danger area to Philip Phlegmatic is his tendency to crawl into a shell of silence when things fail to work out. Since he usually finds it difficult to talk about anything, Philip probably finds it hard to teach his wife what he finds exciting in lovemaking. Consequently, he will silently endure less enjoyable relations for years and cheat both himself and his wife out of countless ecstatic experiences which God meant for them to enjoy.

Philip Phlegmatic's needs. The kindhearted, softspoken, gentle phlegmatic may appear to outsiders as a man who has conquered his weaknesses, but those who live with him recognize his salient needs. These are some of the most pertinent:

1. A dynamic relationship to Jesus Christ that motivates him to think of the needs of his wife and family rather than indulge in his own feelings and solitude.

2. A more aggressive attitude in everything, especially in consideration of his wife's needs in lovemaking.

3. Greater expression of his love and approval for his wife. He must learn to talk more freely about his own desires and needs, especially if the couple is confronting problems. This need to communicate requires his continual efforts.

4. A wife who will understand and accept his seeming lack of motivation without resentment, and who will tactfully use her feminine wiles to arouse him at the appropriate time.

5. A wife who will try to adapt her emotional timetable to her partner's to maximize his vitality, and who will appreciate his strong, silent tendencies, recognizing the depth of his nature and giving thanks for it rather than chafing at his inclination toward passivity. If she starts nagging, he will crawl into his shell and shut her out.

THE PHLEGMATIC WIFE

As a general rule, the easiest person in the world to get along with is Polly Phlegmatic. She loves to please people and will usually give in to her more forceful mate rather than create turmoil. She is easily satisfied and often turns her affection and attention on her children if trouble arises between her and her husband.

Polly's passive personality will usually characterize her bedroom life. She rarely initiates lovemaking, but because she wants to please her partner, Polly almost never turns him down.

One of the most powerful influences in Polly Phlegmatic's life, an influence which will strongly affect her lovemaking, may be fear and the anxiety which it causes. Such a woman may fear pregnancy (although she doesn't have a corner on that problem), disclosure, embarrassment, and a host of other real and imagined dilemmas. One of her biggest fears is that her husband may lose respect for her if she appears eager or forward in lovemaking, though quite the opposite is the usual reaction.

Polly Phlegmatic's needs. In spite of her gracious, kind, and pleasant spirit, Polly has several needs to become a better wife and lover:

1. To accept Jesus Christ as her Lord and Savior. Many phlegmatics have a hard time acknowledging that they are sinners. They act so nice that other people will probably agree. But self-righteousness has kept many out of the kingdom of God. As she learns to walk in the Spirit each day, the phlegmatic woman will gain motivation to overcome her passivity, love to overcome her selfishness, and faith to overcome her fears. When armed with such attributes from God, she can become an exciting partner.

2. To create and maintain an interest in her appearance. Phlegmatic mothers often get so tired after their babies arrive that they become careless about their personal appearance—

their hair, their attire, and often their weight. When a wife ceases to care how she looks to her husband, she has clearly lost her self-esteem. Her husband's love and respect will also fade. A wife doesn't need to be a raving beauty to maintain the high regard of her husband, but her appearance night after night will indicate what she thinks of herself and of her husband. Any man should appreciate the fact that his wife is tired once in a while, but five nights a week is a cop-out.

Some Christian women have used 1 Peter 3:3 as an excuse to let their outward appearance run down—at the expense of their marriage. That passage says that a godly wife will spend more time cultivating her spiritual life than her physical. However, it does not teach that she is to neglect either one. Remember, a woman is the most beautiful flower in a man's garden, and even roses need to be cultivated, pruned, and cared for.

3. To organize her daily life and maintain a regular schedule. A phlegmatic wife finds it easier to neglect her housekeeping chores more than anyone else, except for a sanguine. She enjoys shopping and meeting friends for lunch and, before she realizes it, hubby is due home. Since opposites attract each other, it is not uncommon to find a phlegmatic wife married to a more fastidious man. But after the honeymoon, the phlegmatic wife may find that her

disorganization causes such resentment in her husband and that it spills over into their bedroom life. His uncharitable outbursts may cause a stubborn phlegmatic to refuse to clean up, and produce further disharmony. But she needs to take pride in homemaking. Her husband will certainly respect and treat her better and, even more importantly, she will respect herself more.

4. To appreciate a strong, gentle husband who is a thoughtful lover. She requires a lover who learns how a woman functions best and takes time to arouse her to orgasm. Once she has learned that art, her desire for the experience will overpower her tendency to be passive, and she can learn to be an exciting partner. He needs to be a strong, gentle husband from whom she can draw courage to overcome her fears, and from whom she will receive encouragement. A wise husband will verbally assure his wife of her worth and his love.

5. To learn to overcome her inability to speak the words she feels and communicate with her husband and family. Words do not naturally come easily for her, especially about the intimacies of her love life. Phlegmatics need to push themselves in every area of life, and lovemaking is no exception. Polly Phlegmatic needs to remember the needs of her partner and forget her own; they will both be happier for it!

CONCLUSION

ॐ ————————————————————

One of the advantages of knowing the four temperaments is that it becomes easier to appreciate why your spouse acts or reacts the way he does.

———————————————— ॐ

All four temperaments possess the capacity to become loving, satisfying marriage partners. As we have seen, each has its areas of strength and weakness. Consequently, each is capable of overcompensating in an area of strength or developing a hang-up in an area of weakness. For that reason, it is helpful for every wife to know her loved one's temperament so that she can approach him in the most suitable fashion. Remember: Love gives! When a woman administers love, she will receive all the love she needs in return.

One of the advantages of knowing the four temperaments is that it becomes easier to appreciate why your spouse acts or reacts the way he does. That in turn will help you to accept his individual weaknesses and work with them, not against them.

My husband and I have a lovely sanguine friend named Molly who told me how God used the temperaments to resolve a pet peeve that was hindering her love life. Her husband, Pete, a melancholic-phlegmatic, regularly checked up on her. Each night as she snuggled close to him in bed and warmed up to his mood, Pete would put his arm around her and ask, "Molly, did you lock the back door and turn the heat down?" Though she answered, "Yes, Pete," he would jump out of bed, run through the dining room and kitchen and check the back door and the thermostat. By the time he returned, her mood had turned to ice and she gave him the cold shoulder. This went on night after night—except when he became amorous enough to forget to ask that aggravating question.

One night Pete, an accountant by profession, brought home several income tax reports, spread them out on the dining room table, and began to work. Molly stood in the doorway, watching a strange charade: Four times he added up a column of figures, each time putting the answer on a slip of paper, and then turning it over. When he finished the fourth one, he turned them all right side up and smiled to himself. They all agreed, so he wrote the answer on the tax form. Suddenly Molly realized that Pete didn't just check up on her; he even double-checked himself! She was proud of his reputation as an accurate accountant, and now she realized that his perfectionist trait which made him successful in business was the same trait that caused him to check up on her at night.

That night she was ready for him! He put his arm around her, and she snuggled up close as usual. But when he asked, "Molly, did you lock the back door, and what about the heat?" she sweetly replied, "I sure did, honey, but if you want to check, it's okay by me." He got up and trotted through the dining room and kitchen. As usual, the door was locked and the thermostat had been turned down. But that night when he crawled back into bed, he didn't encounter a frosty iceberg!

Once you have diagnosed your husband's temperament, you can lovingly cooperate with it instead of clash with him.

14

Serving the Lord with Your Temperament

I *could never do that!" This is the response given many times by women who genuinely believe they cannot do a specific service for God. Most of the time they are* secretly wishing they could.

There is a place of Christian service suited for every woman, regardless of her temperament or age. Certainly there are some women who will never be pianists, some who will never sing solos or even sing in the choir, and some who will never teach a Bible class. But for the most part, we are all too quick to say that we cannot do a job—and never even consult our heavenly Father to see what He wants us to do and what He will enable us to do.

Each temperament has certain natural weaknesses related to Christian service, but when the Holy Spirit controls our lives we can say, "I can do all things through Christ who strengthens me" (Philippians

4:13). Let Christ decide what the "all things" should be.

෴ ───────────────────────────

> *God has promised to provide the ability if we provide the willing spirit and the dedicated heart.*

─────────────────────────── ෴

It is important that each of us has some area of ministry where we can be obedient and spiritually fulfilled. When we take in the rich blessings God has for us through His Word but never share them with others, we become spiritually stagnant. But God has promised to provide the ability if we provide the willing spirit and the dedicated heart.

GIFTED MARTHA MELANCHOLY

Martha will never volunteer for a place of service unless first motivated by the Holy Spirit. However, if her melancholy temperament is mixed with the sanguine, she may first volunteer for service and later regret doing so. It is her poor self-image and pessimistic nature that usually causes her to feel she is not capable of doing much of anything. Because of this perception, Martha will probably feel more comfortable working with children rather than with her own peer group. Children are more likely to accept her as she is, while her peers may think she is inadequate for the job.

Since the melancholic is generally an artistic, gifted person, Martha will probably have musical talents, but will be reluctant to use them. Her performances will never meet her expectations, even after long hours of practice, so she will be unlikely to ever share her talents.

It is best not to put Martha in a position where she has to meet strangers, since this may cause her to withdraw and be unhappy with her work. Martha lives in a world of her own and so would not do well as a counselor, or in any other people-oriented service.

On the positive side, she is best suited for keeping records or doing detailed work. This may be anything from taking attendance in a Sunday school department to managing the records for the church treasury. Martha has a very neat, orderly system and often makes a good bookkeeper. Whatever she attempts to do, she can be counted on for faithfulness and dependability. It is true that Martha will not attempt to do too much. But while she conserves her energy, she does finish whatever she undertakes.

When Martha becomes a Spirit-controlled woman, she will have the ability to do many of the things that are difficult and foreign to her natural temperament. I have seen many Spirit-controlled Martha Melancholies become so outgoing and self-confident that they are hardly the same person.

One of our churches had a program designed for welcoming people as they entered the church services. Each Sunday a different couple was appointed to stand at the front door of the church for about 30 minutes before services began to shake hands and greet everyone who entered. I found this a delightful experience because I would never know who would be there, and many times it would be a couple I did not know too well. This is a ministry that every couple could do together. Because opposites often attract each other in marriage, many times one partner is outgoing while the other is more retiring. The greeters certainly represented this idea. Usually one would grab a hand to shake before the person was all the way in the door, while the other would stand back more reluctantly. One Sunday I was taken by surprise because both grabbed my hand to shake it and literally pulled me through the door. What a greeting that was, and it was certainly unusual to find two partners who were so outgoing.

I later learned that the woman at the door had only recently made a commitment to the Lord and it was obvious that the Holy Spirit was at work in her life. For there had been a time when she had refused to stand there and greet people. Her self-image had been so low that she could not imagine anyone wanting to shake her hand. The Holy Spirit can really make a difference! Now this woman has a ministry of welcoming people into the church. And God is not finished with her yet. It will be exciting to see what other ministries He is preparing for her.

FAITHFUL POLLY PHLEGMATIC

Polly is another one who will stand on the sidelines unless pressed into service. She is usually satisfied to be a spectator rather than a participant. But once motivated and challenged, you can expect Polly to do an excellent job. Her dependable and consistent nature makes her a delight to work with.

Since she is a gentle, patient, and easygoing person, Polly is generally well suited for work with children. Children can sense her genuinely kind spirit and will respond very readily to her. She has the potential for being a good teacher.

It is best not to give Polly work that must be done in a hurry, however. She does excellent work, but is known to be rather slow because she is so careful and thorough. She performs well under pressure, but does not like to be put in this situation.

By nature Polly does not get too involved with other adult people, and this makes her appear indifferent to their needs. Because of her calm spirit and her objective nature, she can make a very good counselor. Many crisis pregnancy counselors are phlegmatics and doing a very successful job.

To overcome Polly's weaknesses, the same answer is as true for her as it was for Martha: the Holy Spirit's work. The Holy Spirit can enable her to do many of the things that seem contrary to her natural temperament. But she must first be willing to be controlled by the Spirit. I have watched the progress of one very phlegmatic woman. At first she was very careful about whether she got involved in anything and protected herself from outside influences that might cause her to participate. It appeared as though she had an impenetrable protective shell around her. Even her area of service in working with children limited her, for she felt extremely comfortable working with children and could perform this service without depending much on the Lord. Finally, that protective shell developed a crack and the Holy Spirit got through to her.

It was beautiful to watch the transformation that took place in this woman over the next several months. She completely yielded herself to Christ and asked to be controlled by the Holy Spirit. She even asked to be used in a new ministry in which she would become totally dependent upon the power of the Spirit to help. This is exactly what happened! Now she is out on a spiritual limb that is a stretch for her natural temperament. But she is being supported by her heavenly Father. If He should let go (but He won't), there would be no way she could rescue herself. That is total dependence upon Christ.

Many Polly Phlegmatics have been among the faithful who have allowed the Holy Spirit to lead them to become a prayer/action chapter leader for Concerned Women for America. They have proven to be faithful with a task that is not in the limelight, but is very much needed.

DYNAMIC CLARA CHOLERIC

This lady is very unlike Martha and Polly, who have problems with their self-image. Rather, Clara has an overabundance of self-confidence and has a great opinion of herself. So Clara usually will not participate in anything unless she is the leader and in full control. The incompetence of others disgusts her to the point that she would just as soon do the job herself.

Clara is generally a good organizer and a capable promoter, which results in effective production. Opposition does not slow her down; on the contrary, it is an exciting challenge for her.

Clara's pioneering spirit is a real asset as she begins and organizes a new work and ministry. Her self-motivation and drive will get her started, and she will see a job through to completion.

Very often the choleric woman is the one who volunteers to be an area leader for Concerned Women for America. Because she has a pioneering spirit, she is able to walk a road that has not been traveled before, and she is not afraid to stand toe-to-toe with those who disagree with her.

Clara is not usually interested in being a counselor because she doesn't have time or any interest in the problems of others. She most likely would become very impatient with the weaknesses of those whom she counseled. It is also not a good idea to place her in a department with children. Because of her impatience and explosive temper, Clara would have trouble tolerating the working conditions that are necessary for doing children's work.

She is, however, well suited to be the leader of a committee or department. Some people may interpret her leadership as being dictatorial, but if this is the case, it is only because of her desire and drive to reach the goals set before her. In pursuing these goals, she may step over or even run over some people. So, when working with a Clara, it is best to move with her or, if you can't keep up, to at least stay out of her way. However, the Holy Spirit can soften and change even this temperament trait to make her more congenial and sensitive to those with whom she works.

One summer our Vacation Bible School was directed by a very capable Clara Choleric. She accepted the job rather late in the year after everyone else had turned it down. And when she realized that she needed to work faster than usual because of the loss of time, she plowed into that program with record-breaking speed. I have never seen a lesson prepared so quickly, not to mention all the detailed work she put into planning the crafts and ordering the materials. She had the Bible school staffed almost immediately and, believe it or not, by opening day all was ready and in order.

That Vacation Bible School ran smoothly and efficiently on the surface, but underneath lay the battle-scarred and wounded who had stood in her way as she marched toward that goal. Finally, the wounded rallied and began to drop out one by one. The pastor then had to work full-time to patch up the wounds Clara had inflicted and to apply spiritual Band-Aids in an attempt to restore peace and harmony. He was able to salvage some of the wounded, and the Bible school continued. But so much more could have been accomplished if Clara had been controlled by the Holy Spirit. She evidently felt she had to do it all by herself, and she nearly failed. God was willing to use her strengths to organize and promote, but she needed His help to be loving and sensitive to the needs of others. Cholerics need to be Spirit-controlled!

Friendly Sarah Sanguine

This cheerful lady is one of the most active in Christian work and is very quick to volunteer her services in many different areas. Unfortunately, Sarah Sanguine is not very disciplined and is often late or undependable in what she promises to do.

Children love Sarah, however, because she is a great storyteller. She can dramatize and embellish stories so that they come to life for boys and girls. And since she is so uninhibited, Sarah can easily let herself go and participate in their games and stunts. She enjoys having children look up to her because it seems to satisfy a need she has for being in the limelight.

The church visitation program would also be enhanced by Sarah's participation. She meets people well and is extremely cordial and enthusiastic. Her charisma draws many people to her. Sarah is one who always has many friends.

But it is difficult for her to be in full charge of a program because she is disorganized and usually unproductive. Sarah has been known to commit rather serious blunders, but because most people love her, they are willing to overlook many of her mistakes.

She generally does not give sound counsel, since she is so quick to give advice before considering all sides of a story. Interestingly enough, Sarah has many who want to share their problems with her because of her winsome ways. Many are also drawn to her because she generally takes sides with whomever happens to have her ear.

The Holy Spirit has much to offer Sarah in the way of self-discipline. She already is a willing worker, but she needs to become a dependable willing worker. We have all seen very capable people lose their effectiveness because they are not dependable. One such woman—a charming, lovable sanguine who volunteered to direct the junior choir in our church—provides an example of this. This director was loved by the children, and the choir grew instantly. It seemed that all was going well until one day when a parent decided to sit in on choir practice while she waited for her child. Practice was scheduled to start at four o'clock, but by 4:10 the director had still not arrived. There were 35 active junior boys and girls assembled. I wish I could say they were sitting with their hands folded, waiting patiently for the director to arrive. But that would not be true, nor would it be normal. Instead, there were boys chasing girls, boys throwing books at boys, and girls hopping from chair to chair. Finally, at 4:20 the choir director came rushing in, panting for breath and smiling apologetically as she grabbed the boys and girls and pulled them into their chairs. She hurriedly explained to the concerned parent that she had been shopping and that time had slipped by before she realized she was late. The children later told the parent that this happened almost every week. They always had to wait for her.

The final straw came when the junior choir was scheduled to sing in church one Sunday evening. The children arrived and sat in the pews designated for the choir. Church was to start at seven, and the children were all in their places by that time. They looked darling! The boys had their shirttails tucked in and their hair neatly combed and the girls wore ruffled dresses with their hair curled to perfection. The parents were obviously excited and thrilled as they marched their starry-eyed youngsters down to the front and placed them in the proper pew. The service started but Sarah had not arrived. By 7:30 it was apparent that she was not coming, so my husband drafted me from the audience to fill in as the director. We got through this traumatic experience, but the children's self-confidence had been shaken, and everyone knew they had not done their best. There were 35 boys and girls who felt that the director had let them down. And rightly so! Would you believe that the director had gone out of town and forgotten this momentous occasion? At the next choir practice only ten boys and girls were present. Sarah's effectiveness as a choir director was gone. She had disappointed the children and had probably angered the parents. Oh, how she needed the help of the Holy Spirit in her life to make her more disciplined and dependable!

> *God can use anyone who has a willing heart, a dedicated life, and a prayer to be filled with the Holy Spirit. There is a need, however, for the Christian woman to keep a proper balance of activities in her life.*

Every woman can serve God. We can say with Paul: "I became a minister according to the gift of the grace of God given to me by the effective working of His power. To me, who am less than the least of all the saints, this grace was given, that I should preach among the Gentiles the unsearchable riches of Christ" (Ephesians 3:7,8).

God can use anyone who has a willing heart, a dedicated life, and a prayer to be filled with the Holy Spirit. There is a need, however, for the Christian woman to keep a proper balance of activities in her life. It is possible that she can get so involved in her service for the Lord that she neglects her family and home, or even her relationship with the Lord. If a mother is so busy that she cannot pay proper attention to her husband or listen attentively to her children, she will not be able to do an effective work for the Lord. On the other hand, some women use their home and family as an excuse for not getting involved. There must be a proper balance—we must serve our families, maintain our homes, and serve our heavenly Father.

"Let your gentleness be known to all men. The Lord is at hand" (Philippians 4:5).

15

Challenges of Life for a Christian Woman

*N*ot every Christian wife has been blessed with a Christian husband. In the history of the church, there have probably been millions of Christian women who have been married to unbelieving husbands. In fact, it seems that often after giving a lecture, I meet at least five or six women who ask for special prayer for their spouses. This group of women needs to have an extra amount of God-given love flowing through them. For there are surely times when some of these women wonder how they can continue; it would take heavenly grace and divine wisdom to live with some of the men that I have heard women talk about. But God is so faithful and nothing is impossible for Him. He loves with an everlasting love, and His heart is grieved over an unsaved partner. After all, Christ died for the soul of that man.

LOVE YOUR HUSBAND TO CHRIST

Many husbands have been won to Christ by their wife's constant and faithful, loving attitude toward them. A wife should not try to change her husband; she must learn to accept him just as he is. Some husbands become very demanding and somewhat unreasonable as the Holy Spirit convicts them. So it can be a time of suffering and trial for the family, especially for the wife. But he needs to be surrounded with a spirit of prayer and understanding, and she needs to be filled with the Holy Spirit to remain steady and calm. It is God's design that a wife submit to her husband, even if he is not a believer.

> Likewise you wives, be submissive to your own husbands, that even if some do not obey the word, they, without a word, may be won by the conduct of their wives, when they observe your chaste conduct accompanied by fear (1 Peter 3:1,2).

> But let it be the hidden person of the heart, with the incorruptible ornament of a gentle and quiet spirit, which is very precious in the sight of God. For in this manner, in former times, the holy women who trusted in God also adorned themselves, being submissive to their own husbands (1 Peter 3:4,5).

Understand Him

Your unbelieving husband has a great need for you to understand him and to be his companion, so don't compete with him. He certainly doesn't need a nagging and preaching wife. Rather, he needs a positive and creative woman by his side. Try to understand what makes him angry or happy and what causes him to suffer. Ask yourself how you can best encourage him. Also, be careful to not discuss his problems outside of your home. And most of all, don't constantly remind your husband about God—instead, remind God about your husband.

Please Him

The wife of the unsaved husband should try to be the best homemaker she can be. She should cook to please her husband, and her housework should be bathed in love and prayer. Some husbands become rather critical of their Christian wives, so do all you can to please your husband as long as your efforts do not conflict with godly principles. In doing this, you will be a credit to him. Even more important than what you do is the attitude in which you do it. Practice dwelling on the positives regarding your husband, and focus on being someone who is a joy to be around.

Respect Him

You need to be extremely careful that you are obedient and respectful to your husband. There may be some rare instances when you cannot be submissive or obedient to your husband, but that is only when you are asked to do something that is absolutely contrary to the Scriptures. There are very few examples of this: adultery, lying, stealing, etc. Too many times women reason that the Lord has led them to defy their husbands, in spite of the fact that there is no such command from the Scriptures. Respecting your husband may mean that you have to give up for a time your involvement in a Bible class, or even your church attendance. But remember, your obedience and submission when done in the right spirit will do more to win him to Christ than your attendance at a Bible study.

Examine Yourself

Do you preach at your husband? Can you entrust him to God and leave the consequences of his actions to your heavenly Father? Have you trained your children to respect their father? Are you so active in your church that you are away from home a great deal of time? Have you been critical and cold toward your husband? If you answered "yes" to any of these questions, you may need to ask forgiveness from your husband for your wrong attitude and actions.

Have you ever thought of the other side of submission—of what your submission means to your husband? So many women become defensive when the subject of submission is even discussed. The feminist movement has tried to redefine *submission* into something equivalent to being an inferior, second-rate person. These women only talk about their downtrodden rights. But has it ever occurred to you that God would never have asked you to submit to the headship role of your husband unless your husband had a need for your respect and admiration? The most frustrated men my husband and I deal with are not vocational or educational failures, but are men whose wives do not respect them through submission. In many cases, the man is worthy of his wife's respect, but she is domineering and refuses to submit. Both are losers in such a marriage!

My husband and I were able to observe one godly woman who literally loved her husband to the Lord. She first began to attend church all by herself. Because she would slip into the service and out again without lingering, it was difficult to get acquainted with her. We later learned that she attended our early service and left immediately after so she could be home in time to serve her husband breakfast when he got out of bed. She spent every Sunday with him, "fitting into his plans." This woman was a silent worshipper. She dearly loved the Lord, yet when asked to teach a Sunday school class, she graciously refused. Her refusal did not reflect her lack of desire to teach, but her priority at that time was being a godly wife and partner to her unsaved husband. She even declined joining the church without her husband, since she felt that they were to be united even in church membership. Whether or not she was right in this matter, she still had a beautiful spirit and a desire to be a godly woman.

We watched her continue as a faithful, serving, and submissive wife for almost seven years. Then one Easter Sunday her husband announced that he was going to get up a little earlier than usual and attend church with his wife. It was all his idea and the beginning of what became a new life for him. Shortly after, he invited the Lord Jesus into his heart and that couple became one in Christ. Today they are faithful church members and serve on various boards of the church. This woman can look back on those years of waiting and silent worship without regret. She did not nag, preach at, or desert her husband for church services; instead, she just lived a beautiful, consistent life before him. He later testified that it was his wife's daily example that caused him to consider being a Christian.

Not every wife has this challenge. Some women who have Christian husbands are faced with other trials and testings.

YOU MARRIED HIS PROFESSION

Other wives have Christian husbands, but their challenge is in having to share his time. If this is your challenge, fitting in with your husband's plans may mean you have him only part-time because of his profession. I have listened to many stories of wives of servicemen, doctors, ministers, politicians, sales executives, etc., and they all have said the same thing: "My husband is gone so much of the time that I am left to raise the kids and run the house by myself." There seems to be a mixture of loneliness, self-pity, bitterness, and depression in the cries of many of these women. They feel trapped! This is not about those husbands who leave the family behind to be "out with the boys." Rather, I am talking about those husbands whose professions require a great deal of time away from home.

A visit I once had with a congressman's wife in Washington, D.C., quickly revealed that she had suffered quite a bit when her husband first took office. He was dedicated to his new profession and earnestly tried to do a good job for his country. That naturally meant long days at the office and many extended trips back to his constituents. His wife found herself constantly asking what she was doing in Washington. Even the task of carrying out the trash, which he had always done previously, was a daily reminder that she was running a large house and raising three children with only a part-time father and husband. Her self-pity grew to the extent that she began to let her appearance run down, and she wallowed in a lonely, depressed state.

> *Husbands can be more successful and at peace with themselves when they have a wife behind them who has a Spirit-filled attitude toward her husband's profession and is willing to fit in with her husband's plans.*

The short hours her husband did spend with her were spent listening to a complaining, critical woman who looked as if she had lost her comb and mirror. Her condition grew from bad to worse until she even considered moving the children back to their home state. But God intervened. She was invited to a Bible study class in Washington where she met other wives of politicians and government workers who were radiantly happy and fulfilled women. What did they have that made them so different? They had to live with a husband who was often away from home just as she did, but they seemed to be able to handle it so much better. But it was there that she was introduced to Jesus Christ and was able to accept the One who is able to make a difference. Through all this she learned that proper attitudes toward her husband and his profession would change her outlook on life. She told me that she had begun to count the blessings, for there was much that she could be thankful for.

Several months had already passed since her conversion when I first met her. My initial impression was that she was a glowing, joyful person. The Holy Spirit made the difference! And I am sure that her husband is a much better congressman because of the spirit of the woman behind him. She has become a real helpmate.

The same can be said of wives whose husbands are servicemen, doctors, ministers, or in any other line of work. Husbands can be much more successful and at peace with themselves when they have a wife behind them who has a Spirit-filled attitude toward her husband's profession and is willing to fit in with her husband's plans.

I can write about this from personal experience. During our earlier years of raising a family, my husband traveled a great deal, holding family seminars and prophecy meetings across the United States. When our children were young, it was difficult for me to accept these periodic absences. I could dwell on the negatives during his absence, and by the time he returned he found a pity party going on. After all, the plumbing began to leak, the toilet overflowed, the dog ran away, and you name it—everything that was going to go wrong usually did when he was away. But it was after one of his trips that I received a letter from a woman who had been especially blessed in the meeting my husband had conducted. Her letter went something like this:

> Dear Mrs. LaHaye,
>
> I do not know you, but I wish to thank you for sharing your husband with so many other people. It must be difficult for you to be alone so much of the time. I am sure that you were home praying for him that God would use him in a mighty way (groan). My heart was so blessed by his messages, and God used him to help me work out a very serious problem in our family. You will be greatly rewarded for your kindness and faithfulness to our heavenly Father!
>
> Signed,
>
> A Friend in Need

Little did she know that I was not at home praying. Instead, I was complaining and griping. But God used that precious lady to prick my conscience, and I realized that I was missing out. I did not share the blessings! Not long after that I became my husband's greatest prayer warrior. It is surprising how our spirit changes when we pray instead of complain. From that day on the children and I also became a part of his ministry, and we were able to share in the blessings. And as our children grew to adulthood, I began traveling with my husband and speaking in the Family Life Seminar ministry that I had been so negative toward in the beginning.

A leading woman's magazine told the story of a senator's wife who was legally separated from her husband for three years because of the loneliness that resulted from his profession. She stated that she came back to him because she learned that in spite of all their differences in temperament and goals, she was never going to find another man that she admired or respected more than him. There was no indication in the article that she was a believer in Christ. But if she could come to that decision without Christ, how much more readily can we women who walk in the Spirit learn to support our husbands in their professions.

When we dwell on the positive and learn to accept things we cannot change, we will be one step higher up the ladder toward happiness. The results of the Spirit-filled life will be joy, peace, long-suffering, and a singing, thankful heart.

Years ago, Lila Trotman (the wife of Dawson Trotman, who was president of the Navigators before his death) once stated, "Your husband will never truly be yours until you have first given him back to God. He is yours only when you are willing to let him go wherever God calls him and do what God wants him to do. You must always be willing to let God be first in his life." Remember, he belongs first to God, then to you. The world would have missed the impact of the ministry of such men as Dawson Trotman, Billy Graham, and a host of others if their wives had not given them back to God.

THE CHALLENGE OF BEING
A MOTHER-IN-LAW

For the woman who is a mother-in-law, you can also be a Spirit-filled mother-in-law. There is something about being a mother-in-law that exposes the real traits within a woman. If she is naturally selfish and possessive, that is the kind of mother-in-law she will be. But if she is a loving, gracious, and kind woman, it will be easy for her to be a Spirit-filled mother-in-law.

A well-known marriage counselor once stated that most mother-in-law problems stem from the conflict of two women who are both in love with and interested in the same man. Interestingly enough, one of the most important factors in a mother-in-law's ability to accept her son's new wife is her relationship with her own husband. If the mother-in-law has a wholesome love relationship with her husband, then it will be easy for her to welcome her son's wife into her family as a daughter. If, however, she has had a poor love relationship with her partner and, as is often the case, has developed an overly possessive love relationship with her son, it is almost certain she will have difficulty accepting his bride. And in the instance where the mother-in-law has lived without a husband for many years, it is quite possible that the son has been a stand-in companion for her to lean on for comfort and advice. It may then be difficult for her to fade into the background and allow the new wife to be his companion.

A mother with such a smothering love is usually

not aware of the problem until she finds herself competing with another woman for the love of her son. Whenever such competition occurs, the mother-in-law needs to realistically face her problem. The Bible says: "For this reason a man shall leave his father and mother and be joined to his wife" (Mark 10:7).

> *To accept a child's choice of partner is very important for a mother, even when she may not have approved of the marriage.*

Many a mother fails to realize that once her son and daughter-in-law leave the altar of the church as husband and wife, her role in her son's life will never again be the same. Previous to this time, it is likely that she has been the most dominant female figure in her son's life. But now the best thing she can do is to entrust him to his bride and both of them into the hands of God, while she studiously becomes less and less of a present influence on him. In fact, she should use her mature, womanly talents to support and exalt this young wife to her son. The same principle is true regarding the daughter and the new son-in-law. The daughter must be encouraged to put her dependence for love and security in her new husband instead of in her father.

Admittedly, there will be a time of adjustment for all concerned, but it pays big dividends in the love relationship that can be built between the parents and those two young people. The investment will return, however, through a continuing relationship with the son and will gain for them the love of a daughter.

To accept a child's choice of partner is very important for a mother, even when she may not have approved of the marriage. She must be willing to forgive and forget and then to love and accept them both: "And be kind to one another, tenderhearted, forgiving one another, just as God in Christ also forgave you" (Ephesians 4:32).

The mother-in-law can add to the happiness and contentment of the young couple by being understanding and not making demands. One of the first problems in this area is how and where to spend holidays. A mother-in-law can cause undue hardship and turmoil in a new home by planning the holidays according to her own desires, with little or no consideration for the son and daughter-in-law. In doing this, she risks ruining a good relationship with both of them. Many times holidays become a time of tension rather than one of family bonding. It would be much better to make the times when the couple is together with them so enjoyable that they desire to share their holidays. But the fellowship on a particular holiday is not worth losing the relationship with two young people for life. There are going to be some pressures that leave parents out of the couple's plans on certain holidays. But parents should make it easy on the young people by joyfully accepting whatever opportunities they can to be together.

Begin Early to Avoid In-Law Problems

A good foundation can be laid long before the wedding takes place. Both families can be brought together during the dating days and before the engagement. Planning the events of a wedding with both families will also help to establish a basic foundation on which the young couple can begin their married life. However, it is important that the couple to be married give proper honor and respect to both sets of parents. The Spirit-controlled life that is practiced by all involved will make this a beautiful and memorable experience for all.

Six Steps to Being a Happy Mother-in-Law

1. *Be honest and be yourself.* There is no need to put on any front or false pretense. Your own child will certainly see through it and will wonder what has happened to Mother! If being yourself is not good enough, then you need to work on improving yourself when you are alone. The Bible says to speak the truth in love (Ephesians 4:15). If the truth is always spoken, then you will not need to be concerned with what you have said before, for it will be loving truth. In fact, while I was writing this book, there were many times when I had to speak the truth in love and tell my married children that I could not babysit. But rather than cause resentment, the truth was appreciated and received well.

2. *Be considerate of the couple's rights and don't impose on them.* Remember that they are a family unit now. The man is the head of his household, and it is their

home. They deserve the right to privacy. If they are recently married, be particularly aware of their need for time to adjust and acquaint themselves with married life. You may, in good faith, think you are helping by offering your services, but most young couples want to do things themselves. Be sensitive to their desires and do not impose yourself upon them.

3. *Be sure to treat both partners equally.* Marriage unites a husband and wife as one, and that is the way you should respond to them. Letters, gifts, and remembrances should be equally distributed. One young wife told me that her mother-in-law always addressed her letters to her son. Such a mother stands the chance of separating her own child from her when she does not equally treat and accept the other partner.

4. *Be careful not to criticize one partner to the other.* Just good common sense tells you that this is unwise. One of the best ways to stop criticism is to reject it and not allow your son or daughter to criticize their partner to you. You should never negatively discuss one partner with the other. I recently overheard one mother-in-law criticize her daughter-in-law to her son regarding an unwise purchase she had made. This mother-in-law planted a seed of discontent in the son's mind. By doing so, she runs the risk of driving a wedge between herself and her son.

5. *Be careful not to be intrusive or give unsolicited advice.* You may not like the way they spend their money or their time, but do not tell them so. If it is serious, then discuss it with your heavenly Father and leave it there.

And by no means should you advise them on how to raise their children. You have had your day; now give this couple their chance to instill their principles for living in their own offspring. If you have done a good job, then sit back and let them put into practice what you have taught them. Advice should be given only when it is specifically asked for, and then very carefully. A grandparent's influence can be on a one-to-one basis with the grandchildren as they ask questions and as the grandparent spends quality time with them.

6. *Be sure that your attitude is controlled by the Holy Spirit*. Your attitude toward the couple should be accepting of them as one, loving them in the Spirit, and leaving them in the hands of the Lord. In doing this you will succeed in being a gracious, godly mother-in-law.

THE CHALLENGE OF BEING A GODLY GRANDMOTHER

The grandmother who lives a Christ-controlled life will be a gentle, loving, gracious person who is able to accept the role of being a grandparent. The traditional picture of a grandmother is of someone who is wise and can do no wrong in the eyes of her grandchildren. For some reason, little children look to their grandparents as being special creatures who know about everything. One mother told me that whenever she ran into something that she wasn't sure about, her child would say, "Let's ask Grandma. She will know." Grandmothers are expected to be saintly women with a special line straight to heaven. Now that I have become a grandmother, I realize that just isn't so. I didn't suddenly become a superwise woman with a special spiritual endowment on the day my first grandchild was born. But I am today what I have been becoming and am the product of what controls my life: Christ or self.

It is true that a grandmother can have a great influence on a child's early years. Many children have been led to Christ at their grandmother's knee. Because she is usually not involved in the work and upkeep of a child, a grandmother can spend more time talking to, reading with, and playing with him. Her influence can be toward spiritual things or just plain fun. When the grandchildren are left in her care, the secure, mature grandmother will have no problem disciplining and training the children rather than allowing their wrongdoings to go unnoticed.

This is one area where I feel much wiser as a grandmother than I did as a mother. I believe I was often too rigid, whereas now I am more relaxed in some less-important areas. There are some things that are absolute no-no's for the child's welfare and for the sake of others around him. But some things that I used to feel very strongly about preventing, I now tolerate. A child does need a certain amount of freedom, provided he is not harmed and the rights of others are not imposed upon. It is also very important in this area to respect the rules and guidelines that your son and daughter have laid down for their children. When they say, "No candy before dinner," then there should be no candy before dinner. The child needs to know that Grandma is not going to undermine the rules of the parents. When the mother or father disciplines the child, there is no need for Grandma to put in her two cents. Instead, it is better for her to fade into the woodwork.

The way sons or daughters raise their own family is a real test of how well their parents have trained them and instilled into their hearts the basic principles for living. This should be a challenge to young parents to train their children properly while they have the opportunity. The day will come when they will see their children training their grandchildren either with or without many of the same values and principles.

There is a real need for grandparents to pray for their grandchildren. The world in which they are growing up today is so much different than the one in which we raised our children. Grandparents have a responsibility to not only pray, but to teach those things of the Lord which they have learned to their grandchildren: "Only take heed to yourself, and diligently keep yourself, lest you forget the things your eyes have seen, and lest they depart from your heart all the days of your life" (Deuteronomy 4:9).

The contented, godly grandmother will have much to praise the Lord for. Her attitudes toward life and her children will be Christ-controlled. She may have the privilege of seeing her children reproduce and then her grandchildren reproduce. The joy will come when she sees them all in the family of God and knows that it was the love which she and her husband shared with one another that started it all. Her children will rise up and call her blessed: "Her children rise up and call her blessed; her husband also, and he praises her" (Proverbs 31:28). Another verse that grandmothers can use as their motivation to make a difference is the words of our Lord: "Oh, that they had such a heart in them that they would fear Me and always keep all My commandments, that it might be well with them and with their children forever!" (Deuteronomy 5:29).

16

The Secret of the Spirit-Controlled Woman

*M*ost people don't like their own looks. A group of the "beautiful" people in Hollywood were once asked what they would change about their face or features if they had the power. The smallest number of changes listed by the women was eight, and the smallest number for the men was four, while one woman enumerated 12 changes she wanted. And these were considered to be the attractive people.

Similarly, I have observed that most people don't like their temperament or their temperament combination. In fact, it is not uncommon for choleric women to cheat on their temperament test because they don't like the harsh, forceful traits that often make them unlovely or feared by others. Phlegmatic men tend to see themselves as more forceful than they really are, since society views a passive nature as not very masculine. Melancholies, meanwhile, often respond one of two ways when they first hear the temperament theory. They either ask, "Is there another temperament? I don't see myself in these four," or they respond, "I have all of the weaknesses of all of them and none of the strengths."

Recently my husband received a letter from a sanguine/choleric who had taken the LaHaye Temperament Analysis several years ago and said, "You pegged me to a 't.' And I have been greatly helped by knowing how to overcome my weaknesses. But would you send me another personalized test and make me a choleric/sanguine? There are traits of the choleric I like better." What this dear man and many like him don't understand is that all temperaments have both strengths and weaknesses. The most important thing is that God the Holy Spirit wants to give us victory over our weaknesses. The results of the test cannot change someone, but the Holy Spirit can.

"Why do I always do the wrong thing?" wept a Christian wife and mother who sought help. It is an old story. She knew what to do when faced with certain temptations, but she succumbed to their lures anyway. Naturally, they usually fell in the area of her temperament weaknesses. As is the case with everyone else, her strengths, talents, and abilities were being nullified by her ever-present weaknesses. Only when she learned how to walk in the Spirit was she able to overcome them. It didn't happen overnight, for she had walked in the flesh for a long time. She had followed her weaknesses, and had deeply ingrained habits. But gradually she learned the art of walking in the Spirit. It has changed her life!

ᘒ ————————————————————

One of the best things a Christian can do with her temperament is to accept it as God's creation in her and then, with the Holy Spirit's help, become the kind of Spirit-controlled woman God wants her to be.

———————————————————— ᘒ

What this woman didn't understand at first was the biblical principle that we all have "the sin that so easily besets us." I'm sure you have noticed that some of your friends are never troubled by a temptation or weakness that tends to overpower you. If you look at them carefully, however, you will find they are tempted in areas that rarely trouble you. Why? Because you have different temperaments. Each temperament or combination of temperaments has its own natural set of strengths and a corresponding set of weaknesses. To remedy that problem, God has given us the ministry of the Holy Spirit to strengthen all of our weaknesses. That is why we are commanded to "walk in the Spirit" (Galatians 5:16), meaning to conduct our lives in the control of the Holy Spirit.

Be yourself! One of the best things a Christian can do with her temperament is to accept it as God's creation in her and then, with the Holy Spirit's help, become the kind of Spirit-controlled woman God wants her to be.

Your temperament is a permanent part of you which

will stay with you as long as you live. It will adjust somewhat during certain periods of your life as you mature through childhood, teen years, and adulthood. Enjoy the richness of the strengths in your temperament. Then ask God for help in modifying the weaknesses as you feed on God's Word so that you might become more Spirit-filled and Christlike. Those weaknesses that hinder your relationship with Jesus Christ and limit your walk of faith are sin. Whenever you indulge in one of the weaknesses of your temperament, you can be sure that you will grieve the Holy Spirit. That is sin!

Remember, you are not all weaknesses, though you may feel like it sometimes. Your temperament is the source of both strengths and weaknesses. Your strengths provide your talents, gifts, abilities, and characteristics that God built into you at conception for His good pleasure. He wants to use your life, most likely in the area of your strengths. But because you received a fallen nature at conception, you also inherited weaknesses that, if cultivated, will keep you from ever reaching your ultimate godly potential. That is why you must cultivate your spiritual nature and learn to walk in the Spirit so you can overcome your weaknesses.

After dealing with hundreds of people, my husband and I are convinced that there is a strength in the Spirit-filled life for every human weakness. In fact, we hear a great deal today about the gifts of the Spirit. I believe the nine fruit of the Spirit are the gifts of the Spirit. We don't need all of them in the same intensity because of our different temperaments. But we all need some of them in direct proportion to our temperament combination. Be sure of this: There is a strength or gift of the Spirit for all of your weaknesses.

Success in every circumstance and stage of life is dependent upon walking in the Spirit. Lest I make the same mistake a noted Bible teacher made in our church, we should examine carefully how to walk in the Spirit. One Sunday when this man was the guest speaker, he delivered the morning message on the Spirit-filled life. It was a masterpiece! He had made walking in the Spirit so attractive and appealing that, by the time he finished, he had everyone in the auditorium thirsty to be filled with the Spirit as Paul commanded in Ephesians 5:18. My husband was so moved that he said to him, "That was fantastic! Tonight I hope you'll tell us how to walk in the Spirit." That dear man of God blinked at my husband and caught his breath. Suddenly he realized that he had neglected the most important part of walking in the Spirit—*how*.

The loving God who commanded, "Be filled with the Spirit," has provided simple steps to be followed to make this a real possibility.

First and foremost, receive God's offer of salvation by inviting Jesus Christ into your life. It should be obvious that you cannot live in the control of the Spirit unless He is in your life. And that is not possible until you are born again, having invited Jesus into your life to forgive your past sins. He will give you eternal life and live in you by His Holy Spirit, giving you the strength to be a new creature in Christ. It is the coming of the Holy Spirit into your life that will enable you to overcome your weaknesses.

Please keep in mind that this first step is the easiest, for all you have to do is "call on the name of the Lord" to be saved. If you believe that Jesus died on the cross for your sins, was buried, and rose again from the dead, you have sufficient faith to be saved. All you have to do then is invite Him into your heart and ask Him to forgive your past sins. The Bible tells us, "Whoever calls upon the name of the LORD shall be saved" (Romans 10:13). Once you have received Christ, go to step two.

Second, live in the absolute control of the Holy Spirit: "And do not be drunk with wine, in which is dissipation; but be filled with the Spirit" (Ephesians 5:18). The words *filled* and *controlled* are interchangeable. In each place the Bible speaks of being filled with the Spirit, it also means being controlled by the Spirit.

Take, for example, this verse where it forbids a Christian to be drunk with alcohol (meaning "controlled" by alcohol). Instead, we are to be filled with (or controlled by) the Spirit. You have probably seen a drunk staggering down the street under the influence of alcohol—he is out of control. He is controlled by that inanimate substance. Instead, we are to be controlled by the Holy Spirit who came into our heart when we received Christ. Actually, He is the one who makes the change in our lives after we are saved. I am sure you have heard new Christians talk about the change Christ made in their life after they received Him. What has really happened is that the Holy Spirit came into their lives and gave them a new set of characteristics to overcome their weaknesses.

Notice the nine characteristics the Holy Spirit provides when he enters your life, according to Galatians

5:22. They are called the "fruit" or evidences of the Spirit in your life. For practical purposes, we will call them "strengths" of the Spirit. These are new strengths that you may not have had before you became a Christian. Listed below are those nine new strengths and their suggested meaning.

Love—compassion for others

Joy—a song in your heart

Peace—inner contentment

Longsuffering—patient endurance, perseverance

Kindness—thoughtfulness to others without seeking reward

Goodness—a growing abhorrence of sin

Faithfulness—a commitment to God, spouse, duty

Gentleness—consideration for the feelings of others

Self-control—inner strength to control your emotional, mental, and physical weaknesses

Who would not like to be controlled by these divine characteristics? I must stress, however, that they are not automatic. Scripture, in this same passage (Galatians 5:16-18), makes it clear that we still have the old nature or "the flesh," but we are admonished to walk in the Spirit (or under the control of the Spirit) and not in the flesh, "for the flesh lusts against the Spirit, and the Spirit against the flesh." From the moment you were saved, there was a war going on within you for control of your life and body. The old sinful nature of flesh wants to control you according to your background, your habits, and your weaknesses. But the Holy Spirit wants to control you according to the above nine characteristics. That is where your will comes in. You must frequently yield yourself to the Spirit of God within you.

Our minds affect how we behave, so it is important that our minds be controlled by the Spirit: "For those who live according to the flesh set their minds on the things of the flesh, but those who live according to the Spirit, the things of the Spirit" (Romans 8:5). To mind the things of the flesh leads to death and separation from God. To mind the things of the Spirit results in life and peace—not only peace with God, but also peace with ourselves: "For as he thinks in his heart, so is he" (Proverbs 23:7). What we are governs what we think, how we think governs how we act, and how we act governs our relationship to God. Our thoughts, our actions, and our relationship with God are all affected when we are controlled by the Spirit.

When sin enters our life, the filling of the Holy Spirit is immediately cut off. Therefore, we must regularly confess our sin to Christ: "If we confess our sins, He is faithful and just to forgive us our sins and to cleanse us from all unrighteousness" (1 John 1:9).

One of the keys to the Spirit-controlled life is to immediately follow your sin with confession. As soon as you realize something you have done, felt, or

thought is sin, confess your sin and you will be restored. Many Christians get discouraged at this point
and remain in their sinful ways, but this only rein-
forces the habit. Or many Christians mistakenly think
they have to wait until they are in church next Sunday
to confess their sin. The Bible teaches that, as a Christian, you are "the temple of God." That is, the Holy
Spirit is in your life and is always with you. You can
turn to Him for confession, prayer, or help at any time,
no matter where you are. However, you must revise
your old way of thinking by replacing your old thoughts
with God's thoughts.

Third, read the Word regularly. It is interesting to
note the comparison of the Spirit-filled life and the
Word-filled life.

Results of Spirit-filled Life (Ephesians
5:18-21)
1. Joyous heart
2. Thankful spirit
3. Submissive attitude

Results of Word-filled Life (Colossians
3:16-18)
1. Joyous heart
2. Thankful spirit
3. Submissive attitude

Obviously, if you are going to walk in the control of
the Spirit, you must know the mind of the Spirit. This
is not derived by visions or revelations, but by studying the Word of God. The Bible says in Philippians 2:5,

"Let this mind be in you which was in Christ Jesus." How can you let His mind be in you? By reading and memorizing passages from the Bible. The Bible also tells us to "let the Word of God dwell in you *richly*"— meaning to read, study, meditate on, and memorize the Word of God. The more a woman has the Word of God in her mind, the easier it is for her to think godly thoughts and to have godly emotions and desires.

Most women who have come to me for help were not controlled by the Spirit and were not regularly feeding on the Word of God. You may not have an hour to spend reading the Bible each day, but start by spending at least 15 minutes daily reading the Word in order to grow and walk in the Spirit. Just as looking in the mirror each morning is important for good physical grooming, so looking into the mirror of God's Word is important for daily spiritual grooming. You must develop a daily sensitivity to not grieve the Holy Spirit in your attitudes. This will probably follow a temperament pattern. The phlegmatic and the melancholic tend to sin against the Spirit by worry, anxiety, and fear. The sanguine and choleric grieve the Spirit more through expressions of anger, bitterness, and hostility:

> And do not grieve the Holy Spirit of God, by whom you were sealed for the day of redemption. Let all bitterness, wrath, anger, clamor, and evil speaking be put away from you, with all malice. And be kind to one another, tenderhearted, forgiving one another, just as God in Christ forgave you (Ephesians 4:30-32).

Upon appointing his son John Quincy Adams as our nation's first ambassador to Russia, our second president, John Adams, gave some very wise advice. President Adams told his son, who later would become the fifth president of the United States, that he should read four or five chapters of the Bible each day because it had helped him think clearly throughout the day. The father also told his son that it only took about an hour of his time.

Reading Suggestion: Just recommending that you maintain a daily habit of reading the Word of God is not enough. I find that many women stumble around trying to find "just the right passage to read," and end up wasting half of their time. I would like to suggest some reading techniques that have proven to be extremely helpful. First of all, buy an inexpensive spiral notebook about the size of your favorite Bible. Keep it by your Bible and make daily entries into it as a spiritual diary or journal of some special message you received from God's Word that day. After a few weeks, your journal will make excellent reading for review.

I recommend that you start with the New Testament, preferably Paul's short epistles: Ephesians, Galatians, Colossians, Philippians. In fact, one of the best ways to condition your mind to the Word of God is to read an entire book of four or five chapters every day for 30 days. By the end of that month, you will really know that book. Remember, these books were written to individual churches. For many of those Christians, that was the only Bible they had for a long time.

Then read the Bible for personal needs. If you tend to be discouraged, depressed, or lose your joy, read the little book of Philippians every day for 30 days. If you lack assurance of your salvation, read 1 John every day for 30 days (it only has five chapters). If you tend to be an angry Christian, read the book of Ephesians each day for a month. If fear or "the blahs" plague your thoughts, read James for 30 days. You can do the same with 1 and 2 Peter, Paul's other epistles, and even the Gospels by dividing them into groups of four or five chapters each. For additional suggestions, read my husband's book *How to Study the Bible for Yourself* (Harvest House Publishers). Another very helpful book that will assist your prayer life and daily reading schedule is *Strength for the Coming Days*. It has a daily program for reading the Bible, prayer-time ideas, and even suggestions for memorization of Scripture. This book can be purchased from the Concerned Women for America national office.

A dedicated Christian woman once confessed to me that she was deteriorating rapidly in her Christian life. I had always thought of her as extremely outgoing, attractive, and gracious in spirit. She had been the instrument God used to lead her husband and her three teenage children to Christ. But through her tears, she told quite a different story: "For the past few months my nerves have been on edge. I snap at my husband, yell at my children, and the other day I got so mad I stomped my foot and swore. That's the way I used to act before I became a Christian."

When I asked her what was the most traumatic experience she had gone through in the past few months, she hesitantly answered, "Learning that my husband has had an affair." Her melancholic husband's conscience had become so sensitive after his conversion that he had felt compelled to admit his infidelity to her.

Interestingly enough, she had forgiven her husband. She realized that his sin had been cleansed by the blood of Christ, and so had accepted his promise that he would never see the woman again. Her husband was not the difficulty—the problem was that she knew the woman! In fact, the woman was an old family friend and a professing Christian with whom she had once prayed for her husband's salvation. Now every time she thought of that woman, she would get angry. "The very idea of her betraying my trust and friendship really irritates me," she said. As she made that statement, I noticed she grew tense and her hand began to tremble. Calling attention to her trembling hand, I commented, "That woman really gets to you, doesn't she?" At that she exploded with fury and ended up sobbing.

> *Walking in the Spirit is based on the personal relationship we maintain with God. Our relationship to Him is truly the key to how we get along with everyone else.*

By this time it was obvious even to her that bitterness and hate were consuming her and that she had to do something about it. We examined a few verses on forgiveness (Matthew 6:14, for example), and she was ready to confess her hatred for this woman to God. Gradually she began to "forget those things that are behind" and began to read the Word as she walked in the Spirit. Today, she is once again that radiant Christian of former days because she no longer grieves the Holy Spirit with the attitude of her heart.

If you can walk in the Spirit in your mental and spiritual attitudes, you will walk in the Spirit in your actions. That is why walking in the Spirit is based on the personal relationship we maintain with God. Our relationship to Him is truly the key to how we get along with everyone else.

Fourth, to learn to walk in the Spirit is to learn to develop a mental attitude of prayer. This doesn't mean just a formal prayer given at a certain time of the day. While that is very helpful, it is even more important to maintain a continuous mental attitude of prayer or communing with God. In Bible reading, God talks to you. In prayer, you talk to God. I find it incredible how frequently the Bible teaches us to pray. For example, it says to "pray without ceasing," "praying always." Even our Lord said, "And when you pray . . ." Another helpful spiritual exercise is to look up all the verses on prayer in your concordance and enter into your journal those that particularly speak to you. Then review them frequently and implement them in your daily life.

It is through regular, daily, and continuous prayer that we really fulfill our Lord's admonition to "in all your ways acknowledge Him"; that is, in everything you do "consider Him." It has always amazed me that when I ask troubled women whether they have prayed about their problem or sought God's counsel, they almost invariably say no. No wonder Christians make the same mistaken decisions as people in the world! Christ saved them and dwells in them by His Holy Spirit, yet many Christians don't spend time with Him in His Word or seek His direction for their lives. Some, of course (if they are honest), would have to admit that they didn't want His counsel, for they already had their minds made up on what they wanted to do. They realize that God's will might not match up with their will.

Fifth, it is essential to seek to do His will. Walking in the flesh is easy—you just do whatever you want to do. The trouble with that kind of living (which is the popular "do your own thing" lifestyle of today) is that it compounds the consequences and trials of life. The writer of Proverbs says, "There is a way which seems right to a man, but its end is the way of death" (14:12). A Spirit-controlled woman doesn't seek first her own will for her life, but by faith she honestly seeks to do the will of God as He reveals it to her in His Word and in prayer. I say she does it by faith because her first impulse may seem like a sacrifice to give up something or someone for the Lord's sake, but the Spirit-controlled woman knows that God loves her, that He has a wonderful plan for her life, and that in the long run His way is best. As a wise man once said, "It is never right to sacrifice on the altar of the immediate that which is eternal."

One of the joys of having served our Lord for many years is to look back and say by sight that God's way has always been right. I certainly cannot say that about my own ways and choices. But whenever I made the decision to do God's will and not mine, it has always proved to be the right decision.

And that is what life really is—the net result of all the decisions you have made. Your happiness today is in direct proportion to the number of right decisions you have made so far. If you are not happy, change your tomorrows by making it the practice of your life to seek first His will and His righteousness and not your own will. You, too, will be blessed. God has promised, "Blessed are the undefiled in the way, who walk in the law of the LORD! Blessed are those who keep His testimonies, who seek Him with the whole heart!" (Psalm 119:1,2). That is living by faith. It is trusting God to keep His Word in your life.

SUMMARY

Walking in the Spirit is not difficult. Actually, it is a command of God. He certainly does not make His commands too difficult for us to do. Instead, He promises to supply all our needs. Therefore, any Christian who wants to walk in the Spirit can. If you are a Christian, remember that walking in the Spirit will take three things: 1) regular reading of His Word, 2) a continual attitude of prayer, and 3) obedience to do His will. Is it worth it? Just answer this question: Would you rather be filled with love, joy, peace, longsuffering, goodness, faith, meekness, and self-control or bitterness, wrath, fear, guilt, jealousy, selfishness, etc.? You do have the ability to overcome your weaknesses. And, as a Christian, that choice is yours.

For more information about
Concerned Women for America, such as—

- General information about the organization

- How to become a member and receive the monthly *Family Voice* news magazine that will keep you informed about current issues that affect your family

- How to get in touch with the local CWA chapter or prayer-action group in your area

- CWA's daily radio talk show, "Beverly LaHaye Live"

Write to—
Concerned Women for America
Box 65453
Washington, DC 20035

Or call—
1-202-488-7000

LaHaye Temperament Analysis

- A test to identify your primary and secondary temperaments
- A description of your predominant characteristics
- Information regarding your vocational aptitudes and the best possible vocations suited to you. Fifty vocational aptitudes are offered for each temperament combination.
- Recommendations on improving your work habits
- A list of your spiritual gifts, in the order of their priority
- Twenty-five suggestions for where you can best serve in your church
- Steps for overcoming your ten greatest weaknesses
- Counsel on marital adjustment and parental leadership
- Special advice to singles, divorcees, pastors, and the widowed

Your personal 13- to 16-page evaluation letter from Dr. Tim LaHaye will be permanently bound in a handsome vinyl-leather portfolio.

Your opportunity to know yourself better!